IF I DID IT

PROLOGUE BY **PABLO F. FENJVES**

AFTERWORD BY **DOMINICK DUNNE**

IF I DID IT

CONFESSIONS OF THE KILLER

WITH EXCLUSIVE COMMENTARY

"HE DID IT"

BY

THE GOLDMAN FAMILY

BEAUFORT BOOKS
NEW YORK

CONTENTS

—

ACKNOWLEDGMENTS

OUR FAMILY IS so important. Without our deep bond, we would not be where we are today.

Patti, your unwavering love and support have been amazing. Thank you for believing in what we are doing and encouraging us to keep going.

Lauren, Jason, Samantha, and Michael, thank you for your love and support, and for always being in our corner.

Sammy, we wish you could have known your Uncle Ron. You have his eyes and his sweet-natured spirit. You will always be Mommy's inspiration.

Our friends who get angry when we do, who let us cry when it can't be contained, and who always step in to lend a hand, your support, encouragement, laughter, and warmth will always be remembered.

Kim wanted to specifically acknowledge just a few people in her life who help her find balance and offer comfort: The

Woodgerd Family, The Whitecrow Family, The Repovich Family, The Iacopetti Family, Christine Buckley, Michele Azenzer, John Ziegler, Sharyn Rosenblum, and The Board of Directors for the SCV Youth Project, that gives her the time she needs away from her work to fight the good fight.

~

Our incredible team of attorneys whose passion and commitment to our family has been overwhelming: Expressing gratitude doesn't seem to be enough. We have always told you that your choosing to join our efforts to help us get justice for Ron means the world to us. Your vision, encouragement, patience, personal sacrifices, and business and legal sense balanced beautifully with your compassion, warmth, humor, and sensitivity. You made this happen. You make us proud.

Jonathan Polak, if we hadn't taken your call a year ago, where would we be today? Your willingness to think outside the box and your tenacity are contagious. Thank you for giving us room to feel our way through this painful process.

Peter Haven, for always reminding us to "just follow the law." Thank you for your integrity, loyalty, and for always being the voice of reason.

David "Admiral" Cook, your relentless and "crazy" approach was just what we needed. You are a force with which to reckon. We are so glad you are on *our* side.

Paul Battista, you handled yourself with grace under tremendous pressure; your ability to jump in and get the job done was incredible.

Sharlene Martin of Martin Literary Management, thank you for your immense courage in representing this project. Your heart was and is in the right place to make this book what we hoped it would be. Thank you for working so hard to keep the focus where it needed to stay in order for us to get justice for Ron.

Eric Kampmann and the staff at Beaufort Books, you took an enormous risk and we appreciate that more than you will ever understand. You saw an opportunity to make a difference and stepped up to make it happen. Your professionalism, kindness, and bravery speak volumes.

Michael Wright, you got it from the get go. Thank you for keeping us on the right path and for never missing a beat or missing the point. Thank you for making this process manageable. And thank you for keeping a muzzle on this crazy bunch!

Pablo F. Fenjves, our family appreciates your willingness to contribute and share your insight. Thank you.

Dominick Dunne, we are in awe of you. You have an incredible ability to be eloquent in the darkest of moments. Your friendship, support, and empathy over the last thirteen years have been such a gift to us. Thank you for taking time to contribute your heartfelt words; there is no one else who could have said it quite like you. We love you.

Thirteen years ago, across this country, the public wrapped its collective arms around us and helped us navigate our way through an incredibly difficult time. You continue to offer us that same support today. Your warmth and constant encouragement have been overwhelming and touch us deeply.

To the countless number of families impacted by crime, your pain is all too real to us. We take this journey with you, embarking upon a never-ending search for peace, calm, and justice. We continue to give each other strength and hope. You inspire us to keep going. Thank you for your courage and steadfast determination. We are proud to be in your presence.

—

"HE DID IT"

The Goldman Family

June 12th, 1994, Brentwood, CA

Ron, age 25, single, no children, suffered *multiple* sharp force stab wounds to his neck, chest, head, abdomen, thigh, face, and hands. He suffered *multiple* blunt force injuries to his upper extremities. He ultimately died from *four* fatal stab wounds to his jugular vein, lung, and aorta.

Nicole, age 35, divorced, mother of two, suffered *multiple* sharp force stab wounds to her neck and head. She suffered *multiple* injuries to her hands and fingers. She ultimately died from a deep, incised, fatal cut to her throat—lacerations to left and right arteries and left and right jugular veins.

October 3rd, 1995, Los Angeles, CA

Orenthal James Simpson was found not guilty of the crime of murder.

He walked out a free man.

February 5th, 1997, Santa Monica, CA

Orenthal James Simpson was found liable for willfully and wrongfully causing the deaths of Ron and Nicole and it was found that he committed battery with malice and oppression.

The jury ordered $7 million in compensatory damages and $12.5 million in punitive damages to the Goldman family.

The jury ordered $12.5 million in punitive damages to the Estate of Nicole Brown, of which her children are the beneficiaries.

He continues to walk as a free man.

～

Ron was in the prime of his life, just about to launch his own business, when he encountered the beast that would literally cut it short in a few short minutes and change our lives forever.

We have no interest in arguing the merits of the case and the subsequent trials. By now, a majority of the public has made its decision about his guilt or innocence; however, even thirteen years later people still passionately debate the facts of these gruesome crimes. Maybe the debate will end once you read *his* confession.

We had been through much together as a family long before Ron was stabbed to death. The grief and pain of losing him could have devastated us, but in actuality it cemented our bond as a family.

We made a commitment to Ron that no matter what, we would fight to ensure that he is remembered and that justice would be served in his honor. We felt that nothing we endured as a family would ever come close to what he suffered in the last few minutes of his precious life. That has never changed. We have never wavered. We stay committed to our promise.

It has been almost eleven years since a jury unanimously awarded us a verdict in the civil case. At that time we were grateful that a jury of his "actual" peers saw it the way we did and saw it the way the evidence showed—that he killed Ron and Nicole. The pride that we felt was overwhelming. But as quickly as the jury returned their verdict, he pushed himself back from the table and sauntered out of the courtroom, waving to the cameras as he entered his SUV and drove off into the night. In a blink we were reminded that despite having the verdict that HE DID IT permanently inscribed on the record, he had the power to walk away. He had the audacity to go out for ice cream minutes after being told he was a killer. We were left with a piece of paper that said he owed us $19 million and he went out for cookie dough.

The killer's brazen disregard for the pain he caused, his endless taunting of our family, and his continued disrespect for the system that gave him his freedom—all of it empowers and motivates us to pursue this path toward justice as fervently as we have all these years.

This book project is not the first attempt to hold him accountable. We have been chasing him all this time and he has consistently escaped our reach. He has surrounded himself with a team of "professionals" that vow, as he does, that they will do whatever they can to avoid honoring the judgment. How can that be right? The rest of us would have to pay. If you didn't pay your phone bill, they would shut off the phone. If you were delinquent on your car insurance, your policy would be canceled. If you didn't make a mortgage payment, your credit scores would drop. The point is that there are consequences for our actions—most of us adhere to that way of thinking; the ramifications are far too great to ignore them.

The killer would tend to disagree. He lives his life believing he is above it all and rules that are enforceable for the rest of us don't apply to him. And we would argue, "What else would you expect from a beast that stabs another man in the heart and nearly decapitates the mother of his children, leaving their bodies to be found by a five- and eight-year old?"

When the judgments were handed down, some criticized us for trying to "cash in"—some called us greedy, some made anti-Semitic comments; some voices were louder than others. We struggled with that, confused by the notion that a grieving family, who would much rather have had the killer sentenced to death row, could be accused of "greed" for wanting him to be held accountable in some way. We defended ourselves constantly, explaining that we would much prefer that he be behind bars, but since that was not an option, this was our only course of action.

We heard complaints that we were "picking on him"—that he was found not guilty and he should be left to live his life. Some even said that our efforts would hurt the kids because any money we collect would take away from them. We battled all of it because we understood how much the public supported our efforts and how much this case meant to this country on every moral, ethical, and legal level. But the whole time, one thing remained constant for us—this was about Ron, this was about justice denied, and this was about making *him* pay for what he did.

The civil system could not punish him with jail time; its only recourse was to punish him by assigning "damages" for his wrongdoings. What the system didn't give us were the resources to pursue those damages; that's when the fight began. As we tried to satisfy the judgment, no matter what situation came our way, we were always left with the same two options: Do nothing and allow him to get away with his crimes 100%, or fight and hopefully succeed in holding him accountable for his actions. We always chose to fight. We never thought we would collect—we kept hitting walls every time we were tipped off about something he did or was paid for. It never occurred to us that we might scratch the surface of the now $38 million judgment that he owes. (The judgment increases at a rate of 10% each year. We started with $19 million, and ten years later it has essentially doubled). The judgment has always made us feel like we were playing with Monopoly money.

The reality is that if we do succeed in the collections phase, then we will have real money. Since he is not out planting gardens or flipping burgers, the money he earns will be tainted and dirty because he is using his infamy to make it. It will be blood money because it's coming from evil. There is no other way to reconcile that in our minds. However, the options are still the same—do nothing or fight. Our attempts to enforce this judgment have never been about lining our pockets or "cashing in," or exploiting Ron's death: it is our legal right. But from an emotional standpoint, it is about taking from him, it's about making him feel the impact of what he did. It's about hitting him where it hurts—his pockets, his livelihood. Some people have accused us of having vengeful motives but it is not about revenge, and we are not going to apologize for wanting him to feel a tenth of what we feel every day. We have suffered a great deal and want to see some measure of justice, in whatever form it must take. Sadly, we have been unsuccessful . . . until now.

Leading up to the publication of his confession, we spent many, many days in court trying to collect on a "judgment-proof judgment." Why do we call it that? He moved to Florida in order to avoid paying. Florida is a debtor-friendly state and he is taking full advantage of its laws. He is protected by the Homestead Law which safeguards his house; he lives in a right-to-work state, which means we can't garnish his wages; he is the beneficiary of numerous pension plans, including his NFL pension. All of these amount to millions of dollars of income available to him that are 100% protected from the civil judgment. He has established companies in the names of his children to serve as "pass throughs" for his own gain. He has completely taken advantage of the system and manipulates it to avoid paying. He continues to thumb his nose at us and at the system that afforded him the ability to live and breathe outside a jail cell. He is virtually untouchable and has spent the better part of a decade laughing and mocking our family.

So when HarperCollins announced that *If I Did It*, his hypothetical confession, was to be published, and it was reported that he was paid upwards of $1 million as an advance, we understandably became incensed. We launched a massive campaign to shut the book down and held HarperCollins and Judith Regan of ReganBooks responsible for helping him defraud our family. The precedent-setting move by Rupert Murdoch to stop the book in November 2006 was a shocking response to the public outcry. At the time, we believed that this was a "how to" book about murder, so we felt relieved that HarperCollins wanted to do right by the victims' families.

In fact, prior to pulling the book, News Corp. (the parent company of HarperCollins) had approached our family and offered us compensation for the pain they had caused.

Representatives flew to Indiana to meet our attorneys to discuss how they could remedy the horrific situation they had created. They threw around big dollar amounts, hoping it would help ease our pain. They knew that we were angry and offended, not only at the content but also because they contributed to his efforts to hide his earnings. We called the Brown family, specifically Denise, and explained what was happening. She encouraged us to ask for as much money as we could. "Don't take less than $10 million," she demanded. We took that to mean that the Brown family was willing to become part of the continued conversation with the attorneys from News Corp.

It was over the course of a very long, very emotional, and highly stressful weekend that we contemplated accepting their offer. At that point they were telling us they wouldn't stop the release of the book, but they never asked us to stop boycotting the project. We were torn. We were concerned about how it would appear to the public if we accepted an offer of compensation from News Corp for the pain they inflicted on our family, but then continued to speak out against the book's publication. We knew in some ways it was a PR stunt for them to save face, but they kept telling us they wouldn't pull the book, and this was the best they could do. We were facing an incredible dilemma. He had been paid and would continue to be paid—we couldn't change that. The book was going to hit the stores—we couldn't change that. We were suffering—that wasn't changing either. Would accepting this compensation be the right thing to do?

The attorneys called the Browns one last time and offered them a portion of what News Corp. had offered our family. We received a call from them the following day, and they said "no way." The book was pulled from publication hours later. That move would set new wheels in motion.

It marked the beginning of the long and twisted journey that has resulted in our family publishing the killer's confession in 2007. So much happened between his book being yanked and this book finding its way back. We learned through contracts, depositions, and declarations that he had created a company called Lorraine Brooke Associates (LBA) that served as the conduit between HarperCollins and his bank account. LBA was named after the middle names of his two daughters, Arnelle Lorraine and Sydney Brooke. We learned that Arnelle is the president, and that his children with Nicole, Justin and Sydney, are each 25% owners in the company that allowed an estimated $630,000 to flow into their father's pockets for the publication of *If I Did It*. We learned that his family knew about this book and signed off on it back in March 2006. And in his own words, he said he did it so his kids could make millions. Despite the fact that he spent the entire advance on bills, the kids each stood to benefit from the sale of this project.

By this point, we realized what we had *thought* was a "manual for murder" was no such thing: it read much more like a confession than anything else. That helped slightly when the attorneys came to us and advised us that the best thing to do to completely stop him from ever publishing and profiting from this book would be to levy on it; meaning place a lien on all rights, title, and interest of *his* interest in the book. We were struggling again, but now it was over the idea of owning this book that we had worked so hard to remove from society. How could we show our faces again and justify publishing the book ourselves after we had shouted so loudly about how disgusting it was that it had ever been written?

Again, we went back to our options: Do nothing and then he gets it, publishes it, hides the money, and continues to profit along with his children, or fight him tooth and nail to end up with the book ourselves, knowing we took away his work product, his "meal ticket." At this point, aware of all his efforts to defraud us, the choice was clear. We decided to follow the law; we decided to fight, yet again. We took a very deep breath and gave the attorneys the green light. We're not sure we have let that breath out yet.

The California state court awarded us the ability to sell the killer's rights, title, and interest in *If I Did It* at an auction to be held by the Sheriff's Department of Sacramento in April 2007. Because our family had a multi-million dollar outstanding debt owed to us, we essentially had a $38 million credit card to use to purchase the book. Days before the auction, we were still undecided about what we would do if we ended up with the manuscript, but, fortunately or unfortunately, we never got the chance to pursue that path. Just before we were to leave to attend the Sheriff's sale, the Brown family, specifically the Estate of Nicole Brown, filed a claim requesting half the proceeds of the book. The judge denied the claim and everything resumed as planned . . . for about seven minutes.

As we walked out of the courthouse to discuss our next move, we received a phone call informing us that LBA had filed bankruptcy and everything was off the table.

Of course it would happen this way—of course we would spend hours debating in our hearts and minds over what to do and how to proceed, only to be distracted by yet another move on his behalf to stop us from succeeding. The attorneys told us that forcing the book into bankruptcy court would prove to be the best thing for our family. In that moment, we only felt defeat and exhaustion; there was no silver lining, we saw nothing but another long and endless road leading us to Miami.

LBA's attorneys filed bankruptcy with the hope that the corporation would retain the rights to the book, and that they could just restructure their phony company and publish the book on their own. After months of hearings and depositions, their efforts proved futile. The federal bankruptcy court ruled that LBA was a sham company, only established to perpetrate a fraud. This echoed the same ruling made weeks earlier in a California court that had also deemed LBA a sham corporation.

LBA was a shield designed to avoid having to honor the civil judgment. We had been the only ones who stood to lose in this chaotic situation, and now a court breathed a bit of energy back our way. We had caught a glimpse of the silver lining, ever so slightly. To hear two judges say it was a fraud was a validation of what we had known all this time.

After weeks of negotiating with the bankruptcy trustee, whose main responsibility is to liquidate the assets of a company in order to satisfy all its debt, they finally agreed to sell us the book rights. Days before the judge was slated to sign off on this agreement, the Brown family filed yet another motion asserting their civil judgment and asking for 40% of the proceeds from the book. A team of attorneys argued before a judge in Miami and the motion was denied. Moments later, our deal was approved, and then the judge made a comment in open court that moved us to tears. He said, "The Goldman family's offer to publish the book and turn over 10% of the proceeds to the bankruptcy court is more than reasonable." He went on to say that he didn't feel there was any better choice than for our family to pursue this option, as we were motivated and committed to actively pursuing the civil judgment as reflected by our efforts over the last decade. He wished us luck and we were done. We had finally succeeded, 100%.

The killer swore he would never work a day in his life to honor the judgment . . . well, he just had. He had worked hard on this book, thought he would retire off of it, and we took it right out from under him. He had escaped our reach for nearly eleven years, but not this time.

The specifics of the bankruptcy agreement are confusing. The simplest way to explain it is this: we levied on the book back in January 2007, so we had a secured claim on that asset. When it was forced into bankruptcy court, we had the biggest vested interest, since we also had the biggest claim ($38 million). We agreed to turn over a portion of the proceeds to the court in an effort to pay off LBA's other debts, which included the Estate of Nicole Brown (Justin and Sydney), which is owed $20 million, and a few attorneys who are owed hundreds of thousands of dollars. The ironic twist is that we were now ordered to publish a book to help pay down our own judgment to help pay off his other outstanding "bills," and to pass money along to the family that helped create this drama to begin with. But again . . . it came down to him or us.

So here we sit, having to take on this incredibly controversial book project, which many deemed abhorrent, disgusting, and dirty, and turn it into something powerful and positive. Having read the manuscript in great detail, we are more determined than ever to put this product out into the world as an exposé of a murderer. We recall the language of the civil verdict: "he willfully and wrongfully caused the deaths of Ron and Nicole with malice and oppression." According to the civil code, malice and oppression means "despicable conduct carried out by the defendant, to cause injury and that subjects a person to cruel and unjust hardship." This is what you will see when you read his confession.

The journey to get here was painful. We spent endless nights, hours and hours of conversation with our team of attorneys, literary agent, publisher, and friends trying to find the light at the end of the tunnel. We argued, cried, negotiated, and experienced ups and downs worse than the biggest roller coaster ride, just to ensure that we were doing the right thing. We knew that our decision to pursue this book might not sit well in the hearts of the people who stand so close beside us. We risked the backlash and the criticism, believing that this was a just course of action to take, that this book would ultimately turn his own words against him and expose him for the murderer that he is. We put faith in ourselves that, at the end of the day, our commitment to Ron is the only thing that matters—that our intentions are pure and authentic. We put faith in you, the public, trusting that you will understand why we did this and why this was the only option we had to get justice for Ron.

Many assume that being the victim of a crime leaves you powerless. Those of us who live in that world know all too well that we are survivors and we are a mighty force. We have a will within us that is deep and empowering. We have a need to right a wrong and to make the path less painful for those who will inevitably follow in our footsteps. We have a determination to make our lives as full as we can, despite having a huge part left empty. We have a need to keep our loved ones' memories alive and to honor them with our strength and courage to go on living, despite sometimes wanting to give up. We can not give up.

We have spent years traveling the country and meeting thousands of victims and survivors who walk down the same path we do—we see their bravery and their determination and we are in awe. We are inspired, motivated, and comforted by these incredible people who fight the system every day just to see some measure of justice. We *are* a mighty force.

When we had the chance to write this portion of this book, we knew immediately what we wanted to say. Our first priority was to explain why we changed our minds about the publication of this book. We want to show readers how deceitful and disrespectful he continues to be, and give insight into how we feel about his confession being out in the world. It's no secret that we think he is guilty; we are not asking people to change their opinions based on what we think—but now readers will have a chance to read his version of how and why he stabbed

Ron and Nicole to death on June 12th, 1994. There is no doubt in our minds that this book was originally written so that he could finally tell his side of what happened. After all, the killer was quoted in a television interview on MN1 as saying, "I'm tired of people talking for me."

Since announcing that we were publishing this book, we have taken quite a few hits. We have been cast as "hypocrites" for changing our minds and going forward with the publication. Truthfully, we expected to feel some heat, but not to the degree that we have felt it. Our attorneys have been criticized, our literary agent, publicist, and publisher have received tremendous amounts of hateful emails and phone calls, and we have been the subject of numerous smear campaigns on the internet. We have heard people accuse us of "commercializing blood money," saying that we sold ourselves to the devil, that we are now in the same class as the killer, and finally, that we were purposefully causing Justin and Sydney to relive the pain of losing their mother. We have been called every name in the book and our religious affiliation has been attacked. We have suffered immense pain and anguish and are now having to face critics in the public who once said, "good for you for fighting and getting that judgment," but now say, "you're taking blood money." How can it be both?

In our heart of hearts, we believe we had no other choice. And thank goodness for the majority of the public who continue to stand beside us. Those voices are the ones that give us the strength to stay our course. We didn't do this to cause pain, we didn't do this to "reopen" wounds, we didn't do this thinking it would "bring Ron back," we didn't do this to get rich. We did this because it's the right course of action to take against the beast that stabbed Ron to death. We can't feel bad for a killer. We can't abandon our pain and our mission because people don't always agree or understand. If we walked away now, wouldn't *that* be the truest definition of hypocrisy?

For us, the hardest part of reading this book was hearing him talk about that night. We have seen all the evidence and heard all the testimony, but nothing prepares you for hearing it straight from his mouth. Listening to him talk about taunting Ron and about how Ron tried to defuse the situation was gut-wrenching—but we also heard about how Ron stayed to protect Nicole instead of running away. We were once again reminded that Ron is a hero. When we start to question "What should we do?" we pause and think of Ron.

He stayed to fight and so will we.

—

PROLOGUE

I N LATE APRIL, 2006, Judith Regan, the publisher, called me
about a highly confidential project. O.J. Simpson was going to
write a book for her, she said, to confess to the murders of
Nicole Brown Simpson and Ron Goldman. Only it wasn't
exactly a confession. The book was going to be called "If I Did
It" and it would be sold as an account of what "might have
happened" on the night of the murders. When I told Judith I
wasn't sure I understood what that meant, she said, *"He wants
to confess, and I'm being assured it's a confession.* But this is the
only way he'll do it."

As soon as we got off the phone, I spoke to the only two other
people at ReganBooks who were in the loop. One was a senior
editor, the other a company attorney. I already had misgivings
about the book, partly because I didn't understand what O.J. was
selling, and partly because there are laws about criminals cashing
in on their crimes. I knew that this law only applies to convicted
criminals, but that didn't make it any easier to swallow.

No, no, no, I was told. O.J. himself wouldn't be making a penny. All the profits were being funneled into a corporation that was owned and controlled by his children. I thought that sounded more than slightly suspect, but I'm not an attorney. Surely, if a deal was being made with O.J.'s kids, it was being done with the blessing of the parent company, News Corp., and with powers-that-be at HarperCollins.

Of course, part of me didn't want to probe too deeply. I was being given an opportunity to sit in a room with O.J. Simpson and listen to his confession, or an ersatz version of a confession, and it was simply too good to pass up. That he wanted to describe it as "hypothetical" meant very little to me. I'd assumed from the start that he was guilty, and in the years since I'd heard nothing to make me change my mind.

Not long after, I had lunch with the attorney who had brought the project to Judith. He told me that the idea for the book and the bizarre title had originated with a guy who operated on the fringes of the entertainment industry, and who was friendly with O.J.'s eldest daughter, Arnelle. I still wasn't entirely sure what, exactly, the book was supposed to be, and neither was he, but I was assured, as Judith had been, that O.J. would be confessing, and that I'd be hearing details *only he could possibly know.* By the time the check arrived, we had hammered out a deal. I would be paid a guaranteed, upfront fee, plus a share of the book's profits.

I kept waiting for the attorney to ask me about my history with O.J., but he never did. Ten years earlier, during the criminal trial, I testified for the prosecution. I had described the "plaintive wail" of Nicole's dog, and Marcia Clark used the information to try to establish a timeline for the murders. I lived on Gretna Green Way, one street over from Bundy, and I shared a back alley with Nicole. On the night in question, the unhappy dog had begun to make himself heard at around 10:15 or 10:20, leading to the assumption that the murders had already taken place. If that was indeed the case, O.J. would have had plenty of time to get home, wash up, and climb into the waiting limo for the ride to the airport.

I flew down to Miami in early June, and the following morning I went off to meet O.J. at a Coconut Grove hotel. The attorney was waiting for me in the lobby, along with one of O.J.'s handlers, and we went up to the suite they'd booked for the occasion. We waited. And we waited some more. O.J., apparently feeling skittish, didn't show up until noon. Even then, reluctant to come upstairs, he rang from the lobby and asked if we might meet in the hotel restaurant.

He was already seated when we arrived, and he stood to greet me as I approached. He had a hard time getting to his feet—he had a bum knee—and looked like an older, faded version of his former self, heavier, with an unhealthy pallor, his hair going gray. He thanked me for making the trip, apologized for being late, and offered me his hand. It felt as big as a baseball mitt. He then gestured toward the empty chair beside him, and before I'd even settled in he said, "Tell me something. What is this 'wailing dog' bullshit? You ever hear of anyone putting a man away based on the testimony of a wailing dog?"

Okay. I got the message. He remembered me from the trial, and he wanted me to know he remembered. Or maybe he didn't remember, but someone in his camp had the sense to Google me before I flew down.

We had lunch, and he talked a little bit about his knee, and about his arthritis. I wondered if he was trying to elicit sympathy, but I was thinking about something else entirely. I kept asking myself why he had agreed to write this crazy book, and I could only come up with three reasons: One, he needed the money. Two, he missed the attention. And three, he genuinely wanted to confess. I was hoping for number three, of course, but there was one other nagging possibility: The whole thing was a con.

After lunch, we made our way down the corridor, with O.J. limping beside me, the attorney and handler close behind. We got into the elevator and went up to the suite, and I readied my laptop and recorder. I generally don't tape my interviews—I type pretty fast, and the typing itself somehow brings everything into sharper focus for me: words, tone, attitude, *voice*. In this case, however, I thought taping was a good idea.

O.J. dropped into a chair, grimacing, and plunged right in: "I'm not going to talk about the murders because I wasn't there that night and I don't know anything about it."

"Excuse me?"

"You heard me."

I turned to look at the attorney. "Then why am I here?" I said. "It was my understanding that I was going to hear a confession, or at least a hypothetical confession."

"I'm not confessing to anything," O.J. said. "I have nothing to confess."

I excused myself to call Judith in New York. I told her what was happening and suggested we pull out, but the attorney asked if he might have a word with her. I handed him my cell phone and left the room, rejoining O.J. He gave me a look and shook his head. "I always thought this was going to be fiction," he said.

"Fiction? I don't know where you got that idea. This isn't fiction. I only write non-fiction books. I save the fiction for my screenplays."

The attorney reappeared and told O.J. they should take a little walk. They returned two hours later with O.J. back on board.

He had misunderstood—it was as simple as that. But he didn't want to talk about the murders until later, so he wondered if we might start with the "easy stuff." That had been my intention all along, so the attorney left us alone and we plunged in. We began with the day O.J. met Nicole. We talked about his crumbling marriage to Marguerite, his first wife. We talked about his childhood and about his late father, with whom he had a falling out that lasted for the better part of a decade.

He was smiling by the end of the afternoon. It hadn't been that tough, he said. He liked it. Yeah, I told him. Ghostwriters are unlicensed therapists. "Don't be afraid to cry," I said, only half joking. "Everybody cries."

"I'm not crying for you, motherfucker!" he said, but he was laughing.

The next day was a little tougher. He told me that he had only struck Nicole once in all the years they were together, *once*, and the press had turned him into the poster-boy for wife abuse. And none of the problems were his fault. It was all her. *Everything*.

The term "malignant narcissism" popped into my head.

By the end of the day, we had made it all the way to the night of Sydney's recital, the night of the murders. Sydney had looked adorable on stage, he said, but Nicole was dressed like a teenager. "What did she see when she looked at herself in the mirror?" he wondered.

After the recital, Nicole and the family went to Mezzaluna for dinner, and the press made a big deal about the fact that O.J. hadn't been invited. That was bullshit, he said. He had an open invitation. He just hadn't wanted to go. Instead he went home, called his on-again off-again girlfriend, Paula Barbieri, didn't reach her, and found himself going for a burger with Kato Kaelin, the houseguest.

At that point, O.J. was beginning to look a little uneasy, though it's possible he was just tired, so we called it a day. I walked him down the corridor and we got into the elevator. There was a guy inside on his cell phone, and his eyes went wide with surprise. "Holy shit!" he said. "I'm in an elevator with O.J. Simpson. I'll have to call you back." He reached for O.J.'s hand, grinning ear to ear, and O.J. took it. When we got to the lobby, there was more of the same. People turned to stare, but there was no horror in their looks, no disgust, no judgment. A young couple came over and asked O.J. if he'd pose for a picture, then handed me a camera and had me do the honors. It wasn't the only time this happened.

The next morning, O.J. didn't show. I called his handler, who couldn't find him. He called several hours later to say he'd finally managed to track him down. O.J. was a little nervous about the day ahead, he explained, because he knew we were going to be talking about the night of the murders. "But don't worry," he said. "He'll be there."

O.J. showed up two hours later and had trouble focusing. He was restless and angry. At one point, he said, "You know what kills me? All the goddamn people who assumed I was guilty before they'd even heard my side." He looked dead at me, waiting for a comment. We were alone in the hotel suite, and I looked at his hands. They were bigger than my head. "I'm sorry," I said. "I thought you were guilty then, and I still think you're guilty."

"I know you do, motherfucker!" he bellowed, but a moment later he was laughing. "Thank you for being honest with me," he added.

He scooped up a handful of nuts and reached for a bottle of water, and I turned on the recorder. "We ought to get started," I said.

He took a long time to respond, as if weighing his words. "You know I couldn't have done this alone," he said finally.

"Okay," I said, my voice flat. "Who was with you?"

"I'm not saying I did it," he said.

"Well, hypothetically, then. You couldn't have done this alone. Someone was with you. Who would that be?"

"I don't know."

"We've got to give him a name," I said. "You want to call him 'Charlie'?"

He shrugged. "*Call him whatever the fuck you want.*"

For the next few hours it was like pulling teeth. From what I could tell, Charlie *might* have said something about Nicole that set O.J. off, and O.J. *might* have jumped into the Bronco, taking Charlie along for the short drive to the Bundy condo. And yes, O.J. said, he parked in the alley, *maybe*, and *maybe* he grabbed the knit cap and the gloves before stepping through the broken rear security gate into the courtyard of Nicole's condo. That was a small detail, admittedly, *this business about the gate being broken,* but it was new to me.

In short order, I heard other details with which I was unfamiliar. That Ron Goldman arrived on the scene a few moments later, for example, and that he subsequently found himself trapped between O.J. and Charlie. And that Ron was into martial arts—that "karate shit," as O.J. put it.

I heard that Nicole, alerted by O.J.'s raised voice, had come to the front door, and that her large Akita had trotted into the courtyard and wagged its tail when it saw Ron. That's what they call a *telling detail*. It meant the dog knew Ron. *Maybe.*

O.J. looked suddenly upset. "I don't know what the hell you want from me," he said. "I'm not going to tell you that I sliced my ex-wife's neck and watched her eyes roll up into her head."

I tried to keep things moving, but he refused to talk about the actual murders, so we talked about the immediate aftermath. What happened to the bloody clothes? What role did Charlie play, if any? Who else knew about the hidden path that led through the neighbor's property to O.J.'s tennis court? What was that banging noise at Kato Kaelin's window, and what might have caused it?

Now that we were done with the worst of it, or as done as we were going to be, O.J. became suddenly more voluble. He provided details about the drive home, for example, and actually corrected me when I said I thought he'd driven through the red light at Bundy and Montana. *"I didn't go to the light at Montana. Why would I have gone there? I took a left at the end of the alley and went up Gretna Green to San Vicente, and from there to Sunset."*

He must have seen the look on my face. "Or that's the way I woulda gone."

I asked more questions. No, he said, he couldn't have parked the Bronco there, because the limo driver would have seen him, so he had to go around the corner. And yes, several of his friends knew about the path through the neighbor's property because they used his tennis court when he was out of town.

He even provided details from inside the house. When he was in the shower, for example, *he said he knew the limo driver was at the front gate because the bottom light lit up on the phone system when he rang.*

I'm sure the bottom light *always* lit up when someone rang at the front gate, but I wondered why O.J. had decided to share that.

I kept going. What did he tell Kato about the banging noise? How did the Bronco get back into the driveway? And where was "Charlie" at this point?

"Charlie." I didn't believe there was a "Charlie," and I still don't.

By late afternoon, we were done with the dreaded chapter, and O.J. looked very relieved. It would be easy to say that "a great weight had been lifted off his shoulders," that he felt "cleansed," but I can't go there, because I honestly don't know what he was thinking. If he had fallen to his knees with tears in his eyes, praising Jesus, I might have had something, but that didn't happen. It's possible he was just relieved because we'd gotten through the toughest part.

We went across the street and had a quick drink. I said good-bye and shook his hand, then went back to the suite, packed up, and flew home. The next day I was back in Los Angeles, parked in front of my computer and fashioning a narrative out of a dozen hours of conversation.

For the next two weeks, we talked on the phone every few days. There were details missing. Holes to fill. Unanswered questions. A final chapter to write. He seemed to enjoy talking to me, and once or twice, when he picked up the phone, he'd be singing.

A few weeks later I sent him a first rough draft, but he was preparing for knee surgery, so it took him a while to get to it. After he left the hospital, he was in pain, and he said he found it hard to focus, but eventually the fog lifted and he got to work. He called every two or three days with changes, but most of them were minor, and he said he was very happy with the book. "It's real good. It sounds just like me." Then he got to the chapter on the murders and everything changed. "I hate that fucking chapter," he said. "I wish we didn't have to do that fucking chapter."

He didn't say it was wrong, and he didn't say it was bullshit. He just said he hated it, and he kept saying it.

Meanwhile, Judith Regan had been calling, eager to see pages. She had spoken to Barbara Walters about the project, she told me in confidence, and said Barbara might want to interview O.J. during sweeps week in November to coincide with the publication of the book. I had not known that a television interview was part of the deal between O.J. and HarperCollins, but the idea of having Barbara Walters on board certainly appealed to me. She was huge. She would sell books. I didn't think I'd created a lasting work of art—this was O.J. Simpson's book, after all, and we didn't want him sounding like third-rate Dostoevsky—but I certainly thought it was a compelling read.

I called O.J. to say that Judith wanted to see some pages, but I didn't mention Barbara Walters. At the beginning of the process I had told him, as I tell everyone I work with, that no one would see the manuscript until he had signed off on it, but I asked if we might make an exception. "I know you have more changes coming," I said. "And we'll make them. It's just that Judith needs to see something now."

"I hate that fucking chapter," he repeated. "Ask her if we can take it out."

"O.J., that's the chapter that sold the book. It's the only reason there *is* a book."

"I like the other stuff," he said. "About me and Nicole and all that."

"So do I," I said. "And people will read that, too. But they want to hear about the murders."

"This whole thing is bullshit," he said.

I spoke to Judith. I told her that O.J. had been going through the manuscript with great care, taking the changes very seriously, but that he seemed to be getting increasingly nervous. I think he was finally becoming aware of the enormity of what he had done, the lunacy, even, and it was starting to freak him out.

Judith got the pages and read the much-despised chapter, then asked Barbara Walters for a non-disclosure agreement and sent it over. She called me the next day to tell me that Barbara had read it, and that she had described it as "absolutely chilling."

"She wants to talk to you," Judith said.

Not long after, I flew back to Miami to help speed things along, and to try to finish editing the manuscript face to face. At one point, O.J. told me to take out the line about the dog seeing Ron Goldman and wagging its tail. "Why?" I asked.

"Because it's bullshit," he said.

"Well, I didn't put it in there," I said.

"Neither did I," he said. "If you want to say he wagged his tail, then say he wagged his tail at both of us. That dog loved everybody. He was always wagging his fucking tail."

I did what he told me, but I wasn't thrilled. I had loved that detail, and it's not the type of detail one makes up. Dramatic license doesn't let you invent things. You might recreate a conversation that took place ten years ago to the best of your ability; or you might compress a period of time to speed things along; or you might even change some minor details to make a character harder to identify. But that's about it. *I knew the business about the wagging tail had come from him, but I had no choice. It was his book. I took it out.*

Barbara Walters called the next day to introduce herself and to repeat what Judith had told me: "It is just absolutely one of the most chilling things I have ever read," she said. She let me know that she was seriously tempted to do the interview, but remained on the fence, and I can't say I blamed her.

The next morning, very early, she called again. "Honey, it's Barbara. Let me ask you this: Do you think it's a confession?"

I told her I couldn't answer that—that she was putting me on the spot. She had read the pages, and that's all I had. I didn't have O.J. saying, "Yeah, man. I killed them."

She still sounded like she wanted to do the interview, but she was concerned. She had her reputation to think about. What's more, the network brass couldn't figure out whether the interview should be handled by the news division or the entertainment division. Now that's what I call a telling detail. I myself had wondered how the bookstores were going to treat this strange hybrid—was it fiction, or non-fiction?—but nobody seemed to know.

"I'm still not sure if I want to do the interview," Barbara said on her next call. "But if I do, do you think Judith would hold the book until February?"

"I don't know," I said.

"I have a very crowded schedule," she said.

"I'll talk to her."

When I called Judith, she wanted to know what I had told Barbara, and she seemed to think I'd done us a disservice by not describing the book as a confession. As far as she was concerned, it was unequivocally a confession—because that's what had been sold to her. "I've been telling you: *When they brought me the book, I was told it was a confession.* And as far as I'm concerned, that's exactly what it is."

When I got off the phone, I began to wonder how the television interview was going to work. O.J. was going to hem and haw, and he would interrupt every few minutes to remind people that this exercise was *hypothetical*, and that of course he'd had nothing to do with the murders. But then someone explained it to me: "That's what editing rooms are for."

I also remember thinking that only a guilty man would have agreed to do such a crazy book, but of course that was just my opinion—and it was the opinion of a man who had never doubted O.J.'s guilt.

Finally, O.J. signed off on the book and I sent it in. My editor breezed through it, but he and Judith both had an issue with a line in the middle of Chapter Six, where O.J. felt compelled to remind his readers, as he'd been doing with me *ad nauseam*, that the description of the murders was strictly hypothetical. I had already discussed this with O.J., noting that the title itself suggested as much, but he was adamant, and the line stayed. It was his book, after all.

That settled, I called the attorney and had him come by my house to pick up the interview tapes. My contract with O.J. stipulated that the tapes belonged to him, which is unusual, but not unheard of. The attorney came over and we stood in my kitchen and shredded them.

A few days later, *The National Enquirer* called to say they had heard I was working with O.J. Simpson on a confession. I actually knew the reporter because back in 1978, for a brief period, I had abandoned legitimate journalism and went to work for the tabloid. That, by the way, is where I first met Judith Regan. "I think you should check your sources," I told the reporter.

He checked his sources, confirmed what he'd been told, and the paper broke the story the following week. From the amount of detail they had, it was clear someone had slipped them an early draft of the manuscript.

At that point, there'd be no waiting for Barbara Walters, who still hadn't committed—not even to February. I told Judith that we should scrap the interview, saying we didn't need it, and suggesting it might do more harm than good, but that train had already left the station: Judith herself was going to do it. She said it would air on Fox in two parts during the last week of November, and that the book would be released two days later, on the 30th of the month.

When word got out, the shit hit the fan. People were upset about a lot of things, especially about the fact that O.J.—or his kids, anyway—were going to be making money off this whole sordid enterprise. (*At that point, the fact that the shell corporation was controlled by O.J. hadn't come out.*) But they were also seriously upset with News Corp., which owned Fox, HarperCollins, and ReganBooks, and seemed to have taken synergy to a new low.

The noisiest critics kept going on about the victims, though—how we should all be thinking about victims—and I wondered where they'd been when the networks capitalized on JonBenet Ramsey, the Menendez Brothers, Jeffrey Dahmer, John Wayne Gacy, Albert DeSalvo, and dozens of others sweeps-week winners. I'm aware that there was a difference in this case, and it was a big one: money. But still: Didn't people want to hear O.J. say, even obliquely, that he had done it—or "*might* have" done it?

On Monday, November 20th, Rupert Murdoch apologized for the "ill-considered project" and pulled the plug. A number of affiliates had sworn not to air the interviews, and more were jumping on the bandwagon, so I *sort of* understood. But I couldn't understand why he was killing the book. As a middle-aged man who makes his own decisions, I didn't like the idea of having a handful of self-appointed moral arbiters telling me what I could read or watch. Still, if you owned a bookstore, you didn't have to sell a book that made you uncomfortable, like, say, *Mein Kampf,* even if you hadn't read it yourself. And if you owned a television station, you had the right to refuse to air anything at all, I guess, especially an objectionable interview that you'd never seen.

I was reminded of a long-ago issue of *National Lampoon* that featured a photograph of a wary, wide-eyed dog on the cover—with a gun to its head. The caption read, "If You Don't Buy This Magazine, We'll Kill This Dog."

The next day, O.J. called. "Can you believe this shit?" he said. "Fucking Geraldo Rivera can interview Charles Manson, and what does that do for society? It's about ratings and money. That's all it is."

No shit.

"Well, I just want you to know," he went on, "I was a good soldier for this thing, and I'm not going to throw you under the bus."

I asked him what he meant by that, and he said, "You know that chapter was mostly you."

"Excuse me?" It had been like pulling teeth, admittedly, in the beginning, anyway, but he'd gone back and reread the manuscript three times, asking for changes. If there was anything in there he hadn't agreed with, or that I'd gotten wrong, which happens, I had given him ample opportunity to address it. It was his book, not mine.

"Remember when we first sat down?" he said. "And I told you I thought the book was going to be fiction?"

"Are you taping me?" I said.

"Taping you! Why would I do that?! It's illegal."

He was taping me. He was already beginning to distance himself from the project, and he was setting me up to take the fall. I understood. Sort of. It was over. There was nothing left for him. No absolution, and certainly no more money.

"I treated it as fiction," he said. "I purposefully didn't correct some of the mistakes, because if the time comes that I have to defend myself, I can say, 'Hey look, it can't be me because that couldn't have happened.'" He mentioned the business about removing his shoes, but not the socks. And the fact that he would have had to scale a ten-foot chain-link fence to get from his tennis court to the guesthouse. And he said nobody had ever seen him on a golf course with a knit-cap and gloves. I had asked him about every single one of those things, and his answers, however oblique, had found their way into the manuscript.

I stayed calm, but I reminded him that it was his book, that I'd given him plenty of opportunities to review it, and that I didn't appreciate the suggestion that I had made things up.

"You're right," he said. "We worked together. It was a collaborative effort. But I don't know any 'Charlie.'"

Now I was getting angry. "Don't you remember how it began?" I said. "You told me you couldn't have done this alone."

"I never said that!" he bellowed. "I said, 'At least two people did this!'"

Now he was flat-out lying, but I didn't feel like arguing, so I backed off. Within minutes, his tone had changed. "I'd like to think that during our experience together I never gave you any indication that I did it," he said, measuring his words. It seemed as if he was reading from a prepared script. "I tried to make it clear every chance I had that I didn't do this."

Yes, he sure did.

"I called you today because I loved working with you," he continued. "I thought you were a good guy. I hope that no matter how you went into this project, you came out of it thinking better of me."

He went on to tell me that his eldest daughter, Arnelle, had been part of the negotiations from the start, and that he had told his youngest daughter, Sydney, that he had done the book to help secure her financial future. "The book was very cathartic for me," he added. "I thought it would enlighten people who didn't understand my relationship with Nicole." He then admitted that the shell company—the one that had allegedly been established by and for his kids—had helped him pay down his mortgage and settle his accounts with the I.R.S.

Great, I thought.

He ended the conversation with, "I got nothing but respect for you."

I could see what was coming. O.J. was going to put as many miles as he could between himself and the book, and he was going to use me to help him do it. Maybe that had been the plan all along.

Sure enough, the next morning he told the world that the book was a work of fiction, created largely by the ghostwriter. And it got better. "When I saw what [the ghostwriter] wrote, I said, 'Maybe you did it, because they're saying that chapter contains things only the killer would know.' I don't know these things."

The phone wouldn't stop ringing, but I didn't feel any burning need to talk to the press, or to defend myself. They wrote about me anyway, and got many of the details wrong. It was true, for example, that I'd met Judith Regan at *The National Enquirer*, but we had gone our separate ways—she to build an empire, me to write screenplays—and we lost touch. Many years later, however, long after she'd become a publishing powerhouse, she began to call me, urging me to get into the book business, but I was busy writing scripts, and I didn't write my first book for her until 2001. As it turned out, I enjoyed it. I enjoyed the process. I enjoyed the people (or most of them, anyway). And I liked the feel of a book in my hand. It had a lot more substance than an unproduced screenplay.

The reporters kept calling, and I kept politely declining their requests for interviews. I had been a real reporter once myself, before I sold my soul, briefly, to *The National Enquirer*, so I knew they were just trying to do their jobs. Then Jeffrey Toobin from *The New Yorker* reached me. He had interviewed me a decade earlier, after I testified at O.J.'s trial, but I begged off, telling him I had nothing say, and that if I said anything at all it was off the record. He begged me for one line, and I gave it to him: "I think you'd be hard-pressed to find a reporter in this country who, given the opportunity to sit down and take a confession from O.J. Simpson, no matter how oblique, would have refused to do so."

But even as I said it, I regretted it. It sounded like an apology, and I had nothing to apologize for. Still, it was only one quote—he certainly couldn't build a story around one quote, right? We made a little small talk, still off the record, and said goodbye, and the next day, to my great surprise, a young woman called from the magazine's fact-checking department. I refuted everything but that one line, but they ran a lengthy story anyway. Toobin had taken his decade-old interview with me and made it sound as if we'd just had the nicest, most pleasant conversation, and weren't we just marvelously amusing? I called him to complain, and I left messages for his boss, but my calls were never returned.

On November 21, 2006, Charles Krauthammer of *Time* magazine filed a story about the whole sordid debacle. *"I would have let O.J. speak,"* he wrote. *"I thought the outrage was misdirected and misplaced . . . The real outrage is the trial that declared him not guilty: the judge, a fool and incompetent whose love of publicity turned the trial into a circus; the defense lawyers, not one of whom could have doubted the man's guilt yet who cynically played on the jury's ignorance and latent racism to win a disgraceful verdict; the prosecutors, total incompetents who bungled a gimmie, then shamelessly cashed in afterwards; the media that turned the brutal deaths of two innocents into TV's first reality-show soap opera."*

Not long after, writing in *The Huffington Post*, Jeff Norman said the book's cancellation was "nothing to cheer. No matter how much the relatives of murder victims engender sympathy, it is not the role of media professionals to censor or otherwise punish O.J."

Newsweek actually managed to get a look at the critical chapter: "The narrative is as revolting as one might expect, but it's also surprisingly revealing," wrote the reporter, Marc Miller. *"What emerges from the chapter is something new in the nearly*

13-year Simpson saga: a seeming confession in Simpson's own voice . . . In his crude, expletive-laced account, Simpson suggests Nicole all but drove him to kill her. He describes her as the 'enemy.' She is taunting him with her sexual dalliances, he says, and carrying on inappropriately in front of their two children."

William Tucker, writing in *The American Spectator,* praised the enterprise as "a remarkable public service." He went on: "*Police will tell you suspects constantly come in either wanting to match wits with the cops or wanting to get something off their chest. . . . Confession is good for the soul. The Catholic Church has known this for centuries. Thus it isn't at all surprising after all these years to find O.J. finally coming clean.* Sure he couches his confession in a this-is-how-I-would-have-done-it mode. Police often suggest this themselves as a prelude to an actual confession. And sure he posits a mysterious 'friend' who supposedly accompanied him every step of the way. Guilty people often do that, too. James Earl Ray, in confessing to Congress of killing Martin Luther King, insisted a mysterious 'Raul' had accompanied him the whole time. There was no such person."

By then, of course, it was too late, and the fallout continued. Judith Regan was fired—for reasons that reportedly had nothing to do with the book—and my phone kept ringing. But suddenly it wasn't just reporters anymore. Friends and friends of friends and people I didn't even know were calling to ask if they could get a copy of the book. I even heard from a Federal judge who offered to come by the house and read it in my living room, saying he was absolutely incensed by News Corp.'s decision to kill it, which was nothing short of censorship. His comments brought to mind the famous line, generally attributed to Voltaire: "I disapprove of what you say, but I will defend to the death your right to say it."

After Fred Goldman won the rights to the book, O.J. came out swinging again, doing everything in his power to discredit the book, and to further distance himself from the project.

"We got to that chapter, and I said, 'Hey, I can't participate in that,'" O.J. told a reporter, suggesting that he'd been largely passive throughout the process.

The next day, reluctantly, I set the record straight. "O.J. read the book, *his* book, several times. I made every change he asked for, and he signed off on it . . . (I)f there are errors in the book, it's because O.J. didn't correct them, or worse, he fed them to me. But that's fine, too. It's his book. Self-delusion is a wonderful thing."

You've read the story. This is the book. Judge for yourself.

PABLO F. FENJVES
Los Angeles, California
August 15, 2007

PUBLISHER'S NOTE

This is an exact replication
of the original *If I Did It* manuscript.

1

THE LUCKIEST GUY
IN THE WORLD

I'M GOING TO tell you a story you've never heard before, because no one knows this story the way I know it. It takes place on the night of June 12, 1994, and it concerns the murder of my ex-wife, Nicole Brown Simpson, and her young friend, Ronald Goldman. I want you to forget everything you think you know about that night, because I know the facts better than anyone. I know the players. I've seen the evidence. I've heard the theories. And, of course, I've read all the stories: That I did it. That I did it but I don't *know* I did it. That I can no longer tell fact from fiction. That I wake up in the middle of the night, consumed by guilt, screaming.

Man, they even had me wondering, *What if I did it?*

Well, sit back, people. The things I know, and the things I believe, you can't even *imagine*. And I'm going to share them with you. Because the story you know, or *think* you know— that's not the story. Not even close. This is one story the whole world got wrong.

First, though, for those of you who don't me, my name is Orenthal James Simpson—"O.J." to most people. Many years ago, a lifetime ago, really, I was a pretty good football player. I set a few NCAA records, won the Heisman trophy, and was named the American Football Conference's Most Valuable Player three times. When I retired from football, in 1978, I went to work for NBC, as a football analyst, and in the years ahead I was inducted into both the College Football Hall of Fame and the Pro Football Hall of Fame.

I did a little acting, too, and for a number of years I was a pitch-man for Hertz, the rental car people. Some of you might remember me from the television spots: I was always running late, pressed for time, leaping over fences and cars and piles of luggage to catch my flight. If you don't see the irony in that, you will.

All of that was a long time ago, though, a lifetime ago, as I said—all of that was before the fall. And as I sit here now, trying to tell my story, I'm having a tough time knowing where to begin. Still, I've heard it said that all stories are basically love stories, and my story is no exception. This is a love story, too. And, like a lot of love stories, it doesn't have a happy ending.

Let me take you back a few years, to the summer of 1977. I was married then, to my first wife, Marguerite, and we were about to celebrate our tenth wedding anniversary, but it was not a good time for us. Marguerite and I had been on shaky ground for a number of years, and at one point had actually separated, but we reconciled for the sake of our two kids, Arnelle, then nine, and Jason, seven. A few months into it, though, while Marguerite and I were in the middle of dinner, she set down her fork and gave me a hard look.

"What?" I asked.

"This isn't working," she said. "And I'm five months' pregnant."

I knew the marriage wasn't working, but the news of the pregnancy was a real shock.

We finished dinner in silence—we were at the house on Rockingham, in Brentwood—and after dinner went to bed, still silent. I lay there in the dark, thinking about the unborn baby. I knew Marguerite would never consider an abortion, and it made for a very strange situation: The youngest Simpson would be joining a family that had already fallen apart.

In the morning, I told Marguerite that I was going to go to the mountains for a night or two, to think things through, and I packed a small bag and took off.

On my way out of town, I stopped at a Beverly Hills jewelry store to pick out an anniversary present for her—we'd been married a decade earlier, on June 24, 1967—then paid for it and left. As I made my way down the street, heading back to my car, I ran into a guy I knew, and we went off to have breakfast at The Daisy, a couple of blocks away. We found a quiet, corner table, and our young waitress came over. She was a stunner: Blonde, slim, and bright-eyed, with a smile that could knock a man over.

"Who are you?" I asked.

"Nicole."

"Nicole what?"

"Nicole Brown."

"How come I've never seen you before?"

"I just started here," she said, laughing.

She was from Dana Point, she told me, about an hour south of Los Angeles, and she'd come up for the summer to make a few bucks.

"How old are you?" I asked.

"I just turned eighteen last month," she said. "On May 19."

"I'm sorry I missed your birthday," I said.

She smiled that bright smile again. "Me, too," she said.

After breakfast, I made the two-hour drive to Lake Arrowhead, and I spent the night up there, thinking about my failing marriage, and trying not to think about the gorgeous young waitress who had served me breakfast. When I got back from the mountains, I went home, having resolved absolutely nothing, and a few nights later I went back to The Daisy. Nicole was there, and I took her aside. "I want you to know that I'm married, but that my marriage is ending," I said. "So, you know—I'm still technically a 'married man.' I don't know if that bothers you, but if it does I'm just letting you know that things are going to change soon."

"Is that the truth?" she asked.

"It's the truth," I said.

Later that same night, I stopped by her apartment, on Wilshire Boulevard, and took her to a party. By the end of the evening, I was hooked.

That was in June, 1977. For the next month, I saw her almost every single day, until it was time to leave for football. I missed her, and I spoke to her constantly. I also spoke to Marguerite, of course, to see how the kids were doing, and to make sure the pregnancy was going okay, but I was pretty confused. I had a wife back home, with a third kid on the way, and I was already falling in love with another woman.

I came home in time for the delivery of the baby, but split almost immediately after to rejoin the Buffalo Bills, the team I was playing with back then. When football season ended, I returned to L.A. and took a room at the Westwood Marquis, and I found myself pretty much living two lives—one with Marguerite, as an estranged husband and father of three, and the other with Nicole, my new love. I spent most of my time with Nicole, of course, at the hotel or at her little apartment, and from time to time—when I was called away on business—she'd hit the road with me.

Eventually, I met Nicole's family—two sisters, Denise and Dominque, who were living in New York back then; a third sister, Tanya; and their mother, Juditha, who lived in Dana Point with her husband, Lou. I didn't meet Lou till later, but that was only because the situation never presented itself. He knew about me, of course, and I don't think he had any objections, and if he did nobody shared them with me.

Nicole also met my kids, but I waited an entire year before I made the introductions. I was a little wary, for obvious reasons, but Nicole took to them as if they were her own. They liked her, too. Before long, the kids wouldn't go anywhere with me unless Nicole was part of it.

I've got to tell you: Life was pretty good. I felt like the luckiest guy in the world.

The following year, I moved out of the Westwood Marquis and into the Hollywood Hills home of my old friend Robert Kardashian, and I asked Nicole to move in with me. I think everyone saw us as the perfect couple, including Nicole, but as the months turned into years she began to drop not-so-subtle hints about getting married. I kept trying to put her off, of course, because I'd failed at marriage once, and because I'd seen plenty of other couples fail, but Nicole kept pushing. This led to a number of heated arguments, and from time to time I was sure we were finished, but we survived—mostly because Nicole had faith in us. She believed that our relationship was special, and that we could beat the odds, and pretty soon she had me believing it, too.

In 1979, my divorce from Marguerite became final, and Marguerite moved out of the Rockingham house. I was making arrangements to put the place on the market, but Nicole talked me out of it. "This is a beautiful place," she said. "All it needs is a little fixing up."

She walked me through the house, room to room, telling me what we could change, and how it would look, and it was obvious that she had an eye for that kind of thing. She ended up redesigning and redecorating the whole place, top to bottom, and it turned out so well that I encouraged her to become a licensed interior decorator. Within a year, she was working professionally.

She was happy. Sort of. The fact is, we still weren't married, and I couldn't go a week without hearing about it: *Didn't I love her? Didn't we have a future? Couldn't we have children now, while she was still young enough to enjoy them?* These little discussions often ended in arguments, and I absolutely dreaded them. Nicole had a real temper on her, and I'd seen her get physical when she was angry, so sometimes I just left the house and waited for the storm to blow over.

Finally, in 1983, we got engaged. We had a big party, and Nicole seemed very happy, but it didn't last. Within a few weeks she was pushing me to set a date for the wedding. "I'm tired of being your girlfriend," she kept saying. "I want to get married and have children. I've been helping you raise your own kids all this time, and I love them, but I think it'd be nice to have a few of our own."

The woman had a point, but I just wasn't ready to commit, and it wore her down.

One night in 1984, we were in the middle of another argument, and I went outside to get away from her. There was a tether ball hanging from one of the trees, and a baseball bat lying nearby, and I picked up the bat and took a few hard swings at the ball. Nicole came out of the house and watched me for a few moments, still angry, glaring, and I crossed into the driveway, sat on the hood of her convertible Mercedes, and glared right back. I still had the bat in my hand, and I remember flipping it into the air and accidentally hitting one of the rims.

"You going to pay for that?" she snapped.

"Yeah," I snapped back, then took the bat and whacked the hood. "And I guess I'll pay for *that*, too, since it's *my* car—and since I pay for everything around here."

She shook her head, disgusted with me, and went into the house, and I wandered back into the yard and took a few more swings at the tether ball. It was crazy. It seemed all we did lately was argue. People say a lot of marriages get into trouble at the seven-year mark, and we weren't married, but we'd been together seven years, and maybe that was the problem.

As I was trying to make sense of this, a Westec patrol car pulled up to the gate. Nicole came out of the house to meet it, and I realized it wasn't there by accident. The guy got out of the patrol car and addressed us from beyond the gate. "We folks having a problem here?"

"He just hit my car," Nicole said. She turned to look at me, still glaring, her arms folded across her chest.

"You want to file a complaint?"

Nicole was still staring at me, but I could see she was feeling a little foolish.

"Ma'am?"

She turned to face the guy and apologized for summoning him, and he got back into his patrol car and left. Nicole looked at me again. I smiled and she smiled. A few weeks later, we set a date for the marriage.

We got married on February 2, 1985, right there at the Rockingham house. We had a private ceremony in the late afternoon, with close friends and family, and followed it up with a seven-course dinner for three hundred people. We had put a big tent over the tennis court, and hired a band, and people danced into the morning hours. Just before dawn, we had a second sit-down meal, kind of breakfast-themed. We didn't think there'd be more than a hundred people left at the party, but most everyone was having such a good time that they had refused to go home.

Nicole and I went to bed long after the sun came up. We were happy. Maybe marriage is just a piece of paper, but it carries a lot of weight.

A few days later, we flew down to Manzanilla, Mexico, for our honeymoon. We stayed in a beautiful place called Las Hadas and made love three times a day. That's why we were there, right? To give Nicole a family of her own.

Six weeks after we got back to L.A., Nicole found out that she was pregnant. She was so happy she was glowing—she looked lit up from inside. She read just about every book ever written on pregnancy and motherhood, then went back and reread the ones she liked, underlining the parts she found most interesting. I don't remember her being sick once, or even *feeling* sick, and she was never even in a bad mood, which was kind of weird, given all the clichés about raging hormones and stuff. But I wasn't complaining.

Throughout the entire pregnancy, the only big issue—for her, not for me—was food. She became obsessed about her weight, and when her friends were around she was very vocal about the subject. "A woman doesn't need to gain more than twenty-four pounds in the course of the nine months," she'd say, repeating it tirelessly. I guess she thought she was a big pregnancy expert or something, having read all those books, but things didn't turn out exactly as she'd planned. She gained twice that, if not more, and pretty soon decided to stop weighing herself altogether. That was a relief, to be honest. I had no problem with the weight. My kid was in there. I thought my kid deserved a nice big home.

On October 17, we were in the hospital for the birth of our first child, Sydney Brooke. Nicole was over the moon. She cried when we took her home, but I guess all new mothers cry. I don't know if it's from being happy or from being terrified, but I figure it's probably a combination of the two.

Nicole had nothing to be afraid of, though. Right from the start, she was a terrific mother, and in fact she was a little *too* terrific. She wouldn't let anyone near Sydney. Not the housekeeper. Not her mother. Not even me at times. This was her baby, and her baby needed her and only her, and nothing anyone could say or do was gong to change her mind. Only Nicole knew how to feed her baby. Only Nicole could bathe her. Only Nicole knew how to swaddle that little girl and hold her just right against her shoulder.

It got to be a pain in the ass, frankly. I couldn't get her to leave the house.

"Why don't you let your mother take care of her for *one* night?" I'd say. "She's been volunteering from the day we got back from the hospital."

"No," she'd say. "Sydney needs me."

It took months to get Nicole out of the house. We had gone from hitting all the best places in town and jetting around the world to ordering in every night. And the weird part is, I kind of liked it. At first, anyway. Then I started getting antsy, and then food became an issue again. Nicole was having a tough time losing the weight she'd gained during the pregnancy, and it was making her crazy. She would get out of the shower, look at herself in the mirror, and burst into tears.

"So don't look in the mirror," I'd say.

"That's not what I need to hear!" she'd holler.

"You know what? I'm sorry I said anything. But you're the one that's having a problem with your weight, not me."

It's funny, because suddenly I'm remembering what Nicole's mother told me on the very day that we first met: "Don't let Nicole gain weight," she said. "She's miserable when she gains weight."

Eventually, most of the weight came off, and she mellowed out. And eventually she realized that Sydney could survive a night or two without her, and things slowly got back to normal. No, that's wrong—they were better than normal. Motherhood had changed Nicole in wonderful ways. She was happier than she'd ever been, as if she'd found her place in the world, and every day she was more in love with Sydney. I think she also loved me a little more, too. After all, we'd created this little girl together. We were becoming a family.

On August 6, 1988, our son, Justin Ryan, came along. When we took him home, I looked at my little family—my second family—and I felt strangely complete. I don't know how else to put it. All I know is that whenever I looked at them—Nicole, Sydney and Justin—I felt that I understood what life was all about.

I think we had pretty near a storybook marriage. We had a few arguments, sure, like most couples, but they never got out of hand. After Justin was born, though, Nicole started getting physical with me. She had that temper on her, as I said, and if something set her off she tended to come at me, fists and feet flying. Mostly I'd just try to get out of her way, but sometimes I had to hold her down till she got herself under control. So, yeah—we argued. And we could get pushy about it. And sometimes the arguments ended with Nicole in tears. But more often than not they ended in laughter. It was crazy: I can't count the number of times she'd turn to me in the middle of a fight, pausing to catch her breath, and say, "O.J., what the hell were we arguing about, anyway?"

Years later, during the trial, the prosecution tried to paint a picture of me as a violent, abusive husband. They said they'd found a safe-deposit box belonging to Nicole, and that it contained numerous handwritten allegations of abuse dating back to 1977. In the notes, Nicole reportedly said all sorts of ugly things about me: That I constantly told her she was fat; that when she got pregnant with Justin I said I didn't want another kid; that I once locked her in our wine closet during an argument. I don't know what all else I did, but the list was endless, and all of it was fiction. And if it's true that those handwritten notes were from Nicole, and that they were really found in her safe-deposit box, and that she really was making those allegations, well—I still say it was fiction, still maintain that these incidents existed only in Nicole's own mind. I honestly can't make any sense of it. I've tried, though. At one point I wondered if she started working on those notes when the marriage began to go south. Maybe she thought she could use them against me if it ever came to divorce, which makes me wonder: Why *didn't* she use them? I don't know what she was thinking, frankly, but if any of those things happened I wasn't around when they did. And, yeah, I know: It sounds cruel here, on the page, with Nicole gone and everything, unable to defend herself, but I said I would tell the truth, and that's what I intend to do.

Did things get volatile from time to time? Yes. Do I regret it? Yes. I loved Nicole. She was the mother of two of my kids, and the last thing I wanted was to hurt her. I only ever got truly physical with her once, and that was in 1989—and the whole world heard about it.

Let me take you back. It was New Year's Eve. Nicole and I

were at a party early in the evening, at the home of a producer friend, hanging out with Marcus Allen, one of my old football buddies, and his girlfriend, Kathryn. Marcus had bought some expensive earrings for Kathryn, as a little New Year's present, and I guess Nicole got a little jealous. Kathryn couldn't see what she was jealous about, though, since Nicole was dripping in diamonds of her own, and she spelled it out for her: "Well, look what *you* got, girl!" I don't know what Nicole was thinking, but for some reason she got it into her head that a pair of earrings—just like Kathryn's—were waiting for her back at the house. And of course there were no earrings. We got home after the party, and we were in bed, making love, and suddenly Nicole sat up and looked at me.

"You have a little surprise for me?" she said, smiling coyly.

"What surprise?"

"Diamond earrings maybe?"

"What earrings?" I said, getting irritated.

"Like the ones Marcus got Kathryn," she said.

"What the hell are you talking about?"

"Kathryn said you bought a pair of earrings just like the ones she was wearing. Where are they? If you didn't get them for me, who'd you get them for?"

And I said, "You're crazy! I didn't get nobody no damn earrings. And I'm not about to, either." I'm sure that was the wrong thing to say, but I was angry, and my anger set her off. She took a swing at me and I grabbed her arm and literally dragged her out of bed and pulled her toward the door.

"Where are the goddamn earrings?!" she hollered, still taking swings at me.

"There are no earrings!" I snapped back.

"Liar! Who'd you give the earrings to?!"

"I didn't give any goddamn earrings to anybody!" I said.

"There are no earrings! Now get out of here. I don't want you in my bedroom."

I pushed her into the corridor and locked her out, then went back to bed, still fuming. I didn't know what the hell was going on with Nicole. She was becoming increasingly erratic. Most of the time she was a loving wife and a perfect mother, but it seemed like lately any little thing could set her off. To be honest, it worried me. There we were, two in the goddamn morning, and she was standing out in the corridor, banging on the door, hollering. It was as if she had turned into a whole different person. Finally, she gave up, and I could hear her moving off. There were plenty of other bedrooms in the house. Nicole could sleep alone if she was going to be like that.

A minute later, she was back. Turned out she'd only gone to get the key, and there she was, coming at me all over again, fists and feet flying. So I grabbed her, *again*, and I threw her out, *again*, and this time I kept the key.

"Let me in, you bastard!"

"No! Go away!"

I went back to bed and rolled on my side and pulled the covers over my head, wondering if something was wrong with my wife. We'd been together for twelve years, and in many ways they'd been the twelve best years of my life, but it seemed like most of 1989 had been torture. You never knew what was going to piss her off, and when she was pissed off she could hold onto her anger for *days*. I wondered how long she was going to stay angry this time. She kept pounding on the door, swearing and calling me names, and I worried that she would wake the kids, but eventually the fight went out of her and she stormed off.

I don't know how much time passed, because I dozed off, but suddenly she was at the door again. Only it wasn't her. It was the housekeeper, Michele. "Mr. Simpson," she said, trying to make herself heard through the door. "You have to come outside. The police are here."

The police? What the hell?

I pulled on a pair of pants and went downstairs and out the front door and found Nicole sitting in a patrol car that was parked in front of the house. "What's going on?" I asked.

I saw Nicole trying to get out of the car, and I could hear the cops telling her to sit still. Michele was standing right behind me, and she saw it, too. "Come on, Miss Nicole," she called out. "Everything's going to be all right. Come back inside."

Suddenly Nicole was crying. "My baby's in the house," she said. "I want my baby back."

"Well, *come on*," I said. "What's keeping you?"

Michele tried, too. "Please come in the house, Miss Nicole," she said. "Everything's fine now."

One of the cops turned to look at Michele, scowling. "Why don't you mind your own business," he said.

"Hey," I snapped. "You got no right to talk to my housekeeper that way!"

"She should mind her own business," he said.

I couldn't believe the guy. He was parked in front of my property, talking shit to my housekeeper, and telling me how to run my personal affairs. "Man, you don't have a right to talk to *either* of us that way," I said. I was seriously pissed by this time, and I was seriously tired, and I didn't want to do anything stupid, so I turned to Michele and led her back into the house. I figured Nicole would come back when she was good and ready.

But Nicole didn't come back for several hours. She went down to the precinct with the cops and they took a statement from her and had her pose for pictures. It was three in the morning by then. She was drunk, she'd been crying, and she was under fluorescent lights without any makeup. Ask me how bad she looked?

Then they took her to the hospital and the doctors gave her the once-over. In their report, which I only read much later, they noted that there were bruises on her face and arms. That was about it. I could have told them about the bruises. The ones on her arms—I put them there. Her face? I didn't hit her, but it's possible she hurt herself while we were scuffling.

Years later, during the murder trial, I found out that one of the officers who responded that night was a man by the name of John Edwards. He testified that Nicole had bruises on her forehead, cuts on her nose and cheek, and a handprint on her neck. I don't remember any of that, and if it was there I didn't see it. Edwards quoted Nicole as saying, "You guys come out here, you talk to him, you leave. You've been out here eight times, I want him arrested, and I want my kids back."

Eight times? What the hell was she talking about? And what was that about wanting her kids back? Back from *what?* From *where?* All I heard was, "My baby's in the house. I want my baby back." I wasn't stopping her. From where I was standing, the only thing keeping her from getting out of the patrol car and marching back into the house were the damn cops.

Edwards also said I screamed at Nicole: "I got two other women! I don't want that woman in my bed anymore!" I don't remember saying anything about not wanting Nicole in my bed anymore, but at that moment it was sure as hell true. I didn't want her anywhere *near* me. The part about the "two other women," though—Edwards got that completely wrong. I was talking about the two women *in the house*—the nanny and the housekeeper—because Nicole seemed to be concerned about the baby, and I was just letting her know that the baby was in good hands.

I guess she got the message, because she split and didn't come home till just before daybreak. When she walked through the front door, I looked at her and felt lousy. "I never meant to hurt you," I said. "I just wanted you out of the bedroom."

"I have a headache," she said.

"You want me to take you to the hospital?"

"No. It's probably just a hangover."

"Maybe it's a concussion," I said. "I don't mind taking you."

"Just leave me alone," she said. "I'm sick of this."

I was sick of it too, frankly. I went off and spent what was left of the night at a friend's house, and in the afternoon I went to the Rose Bowl and tried to put the bad feelings behind me.

When I got home that evening, long after the Rose Bowl ended, Nicole was there with the kids, and neither of us said a word about the incident. We kind of walked around each other, not saying much of anything, really, and I assumed that life at Rockingham would eventually get back to normal.

The next day, or the day after that—I can't recall exactly—a detective came by to follow up with a few questions, and I walked the guy through it. I said I'd been drinking—that we'd *both* been drinking—and admitted that I'd become a little bit too physical. "I should have exercised more self-control," I said.

"It's one of those things that happen in all relationships," he said, and I agreed with him. *We'd been partying a little too hard. It was late. We weren't thinking clearly. But hey, nobody got hurt.* Yada yada yada.

As for Nicole, I guess she told the cops her own version of the same story, down to that misunderstanding about the non-existent diamond earrings. I don't know if she told them that she took a few swings at me, and that she came back for more after I locked her out, but she certainly told her mother, who went on national television and confirmed it. Still, at that point none of it seemed relevant. I had already apologized, profusely, and had even gone one better. "If I'm ever physical like that with you again, I will tear up the prenuptial agreement," I told Nicole. I wanted her to know how serious I was about making things right. It didn't matter to me that she had initiated the fight because my response was wrong, and that's what counted—my response.

"Thank you," she said.

"I mean it," I said.

"I know," she said.

So, yeah—as far as I was concerned, it was over.

But it wasn't over. A month later, just as we were getting ready to fly to Hawaii, where I had business with Hertz, I woke up and read about the whole ugly incident on the front page of the *Herald Examiner*. It was surreal. I thought we'd moved on long ago, then bam!—there it was for the whole world to see. The story came as a complete surprise to Nicole, too. She had no idea that the cops were going to use her statement, and those incriminating photographs, to charge me with domestic abuse.

In the days ahead, everything became a little clearer. I found out that it's quite common for a woman to charge her husband or boyfriend with abuse, only to call the police the next day and ask them to drop the charges. I guess they're afraid of what those guys will do to them when it's all over, so they find all sorts of reasons to change their stories: *It was a misunderstanding, officer. Deep down I really love him. I don't want to hurt the kids. Now that I think about it, the whole thing was my fault.* Many women kept getting victimized as a result, repeatedly, sometimes with deadly results, and the cops were trying to figure out how to deal with the problem. In fact, they were attempting to put a new law on the books that would give them the power to make the charges stick, even if the complaint was withdrawn. And I guess what happened was, someone at the L.A.P.D. decided that I would make the perfect poster boy for spousal abuse—a perfect, high-profile launch for their campaign.

There was one glitch, however, and it was a big one. Back in those days, officers could only make an arrest if it was warranted by the situation, or if the perpetrator had a history of abuse. Our situation hadn't warranted it—no one was getting beat up—and I didn't have a history of abuse. Still, just in case anything had slipped though the cracks, the investigating officer sent a memo to various neighborhood precincts, asking if any officer had ever responded to a domestic disturbance at my home. Well, wouldn't you know it—they got lucky. The Westec security guard who had stopped by during our one previous altercation, in 1984, had since become a member of the L.A.P.D., and both he and one of his fellow officers, Mark Fuhrman, responded to the memo. In his response, Fuhrman actually claimed that he'd been at my house that night, with the guy from Westec, and that he'd talked to both me and Nicole. If Fuhrman was there, and if he actually talked to either of us, I sure as hell don't remember it. But that didn't matter. The L.A.P.D. had been looking for a prior incident, and they'd just found it.

In the end, I was convicted of spousal abuse. I was put on probation, given a few hundred hours of community service, and ordered to pay a modest fine. I wasn't happy about it, but I didn't think the charges were worth fighting, and I regret it to this day. If you don't fight the charges, they stick. And these stuck. Suddenly, I was a convicted wife-beater.

Did I physically drag Nicole out of the bedroom and push her out into the hallway? Yes. Did I beat her? No. I never once raised my hand to her—never once—and if Nicole were alive today she'd tell you the same thing. In fact, right after the newspaper story broke, when she talked to her mother about it, she took responsibility for the whole ugly incident. And even during the divorce proceedings years later, when she had good reason to want to lie about my allegedly violent nature, Nicole refused to play that game. She told her lawyers that the incident had been blown completely out of proportion—and that she'd instigated the violence, not me.

Much later, months after the murders, I spoke about the incident with Dr. Bernard Yudowitz, a forensic psychiatrist. I remember crying as I told him about going up to San Francisco in 1986, to see my father, who was in the hospital at the time, riddled with cancer. He was tired and weak, but in good spirits, and we chatted for a while, then I took a moment to step out into the corridor to call Nicole, back in L.A. When I returned to the room, my father was dead. "I don't understand why God gave me ten minutes with my father," I told Dr. Yudowitz, "but not even one second with Nicole."

I will admit to you, as I admitted to him, that some of my arguments with Nicole did indeed deteriorate into shouting matches, and that we tended to get in each other's faces. But most of the time *we resolved our differences peacefully*, without getting physical. Nicole and I were together for seventeen years, and we had our share of conflict, but by and large we were always able to work out our differences.

During the trial, when Dr. Yudowitz took the stand—on my behalf, admittedly—he said what everyone expected him to say: That I did not fit the profile of a killer. In the days ahead, as expected, the newspapers trotted out their own experts. They said that four out of five murders were spontaneous, a result of circumstance more than intent, and that perhaps that had been the situation in my case. I also read about so-called "atypical" murderers: The quiet boy next door, say, or the mousy little preacher's wife—men and women who seemed incapable of murder, but who were driven to violence by a given situation. Some experts immediately categorized me as atypical: I seemed like a nice guy, and it was definitely out of character for me to have committed the crime, but I could have done it just the same. That didn't strike me as particularly insightful. Given the right circumstances, I guess anyone is capable of murder.

But I'm getting ahead of myself . . .

When I think back on my marriage to Nicole, I guess I'd have to say that 1989 was the big turning point—but mostly for *her*. Me? I was the oblivious husband. For one thing, I got busy. A few weeks after the incident, I had to go to Hawaii, for Hertz, and my business with them kept me occupied for the next few months. Then in the fall, I had *NFL Live* to do, with Bob Costas, and once again—like lots of guys—I lost myself in my work. I wasn't even thinking about the incident, to be honest. I was moving forward, leaving it behind me, and in my mind that was a good thing. I thought we should put the past behind us. Cool off. Start fresh. And I figured Nicole probably felt the same way. She seemed a little removed at times, to be honest, but otherwise I thought things were fine. I didn't realize till much later that she was having an affair, but that's another story, and I was completely oblivious about that, too. Maybe it was self-delusion—who knows? All I know is that I thought things were solid, and that I felt we could get through anything. Plus I didn't want the marriage to fail. We had two kids to raise, and we were at that point in our marriage where the kids had to come first. That's just the way it was. It wasn't that I didn't love Nicole, or that I loved her less, but that I loved her in a different way. You lose some of the passion, sure, and you lose some of the closeness. And sometimes you're just trying to stay out of each other's way. But so what? The center of gravity shifts. You focus on the kids. You settle down. You mellow out. And that's what I was doing, or *trying* to do.

And it was working great—or so I thought. I remember being in New York in December 1991, hanging out with Nicole, doing a little Christmas shopping and stuff, and thinking how happy she seemed. She even *looked* terrific. She had been struggling to get back into fighting shape ever since the kids had come along, and *complaining* about it every time she caught sight of herself in the mirror, but after months of hard work she was in the best shape of her life. I was amazed, and I told her so, and I remember thinking how glad I was that we'd weathered the post-1989 storm. I was proud of myself for making it through the rough parts of the marriage, and equally proud of her, and I was feeling genuinely optimistic about the future.

A month later, in January 1992, I was in New York for the playoff games, and flew home for a long weekend. The very first day I was back, Nicole and I went to lunch at Peppone's, right there in Brentwood, and about thirty seconds after we sat down she let me have it: "I think we should separate," she said.

I was floored. I was tired and jet-lagged and I honestly wasn't even sure I'd even heard her right, but she repeated it, saying she didn't understand why I looked so surprised. We'd been having problems for a long time, she said, and we should both look at it as an opportunity to work on ourselves and think about the problems, yada yada yada. "I want to try living apart for a month," she added. "But I don't want to get the lawyers involved."

Then she suggested that I move out of the Rockingham house, to make the separation less disruptive for the kids, and I knew right off that I had to stop this thing before it got any crazier. "I don't know what you think you're going to accomplish by us living apart for a month," I said. "I'm hardly here as it is, traveling all the time. If you want to work on yourself, you've got plenty of time to do it. And if you think I need to work on myself, maybe you can tell me what needs fixing."

"No," she said. "That's not it at all."

"Then what is it?" I said. "I'm confused. Is there someone else?"

"No—God! How can you even think such a thing?"

"I don't know," I said. "I'm trying to figure out how it came to this. I know we don't have a perfect marriage, but who does? And I thought we were doing pretty well."

At that point she began to talk about the fact that she had spent her entire adult life with me—fifteen years—and that she felt as if she was living in my shadow. "All of our friends are your friends," she said. "Everything we do is stuff you want to do. Our life together is basically about you."

I tried to defend myself, saying that I had always listened to her, and that I had never stopped her from pursuing her own interests and her own friendships, but she wasn't really paying attention. "I want to be around people who like me for me, not because I'm O.J. Simpson's wife," she said.

I thought that was bullshit, too, and I told her so, but she was adamant: she wanted to take a break from the marriage.

"Fine," I said, trying to keep emotion out of it. "If you want a break, I'll give you a break. But there's no way in hell we're doing this without lawyers." We needed the lawyers so that we'd be absolutely clear on what was going on, I explained. *She* wanted out, not me, for reasons I couldn't really understand. And the Rockingham house predated our relationship. It was *my* house, a fact that was clearly spelled out in the prenuptial agreement. That house held a lot of history for me, including the drowning death of my infant daughter, Aaren—the little girl

I had with Marguerite during the rocky tail end of our marriage—and I wasn't going to let anyone tell me to move out.

At the end of that month, with the lawyers already hard at work, Nicole moved into a rented house on Gretna Green Way, not eight minutes from my place, and—given my hectic travel schedule—took physical custody of the kids. I was in a state of mild shock for several weeks, to be honest, unable to get my mind around what had happened, and how it had come to this. Her mother was in shock, too, as were most of her friends. None of them seemed to think that our problems were all that significant, though of course one never really knows what goes on behind closed doors.

The only person who had seen it coming was her best friend, Cora Fishman, because Cora had known about the affair—the one Nicole denied having. It wasn't anyone she was serious about, I learned much later, but it had happened, and when shit like that happens you know that deep down something is very wrong. It's strange, though, because years later, in a letter she wrote me when she was trying to reconcile, she still said nothing about the affair. Instead, she talked about the 1989 incident, and how that had been the big turning point in our relationship—for her, anyway—which was kind of odd because she was no longer blaming me for what had happened. She said she was beginning to realize that she had contributed as much to our problems as I had, if not more, and that looking back on it she felt that I'd been right from the start—that we *did* have a pretty good life together. It was the first time she had taken responsibility for her actions, and it was a good thing, but unfortunately it came too late. When I read that letter, it about broke my heart. All along I thought we were going to make it, and I guess I never really understood the depth of her unhappiness—let alone the reasons for it.

So we started our new life, in separate homes but still committed to making it work—like so many other couples. I was optimistic, to be honest. I had been through this before, with Marguerite, *twice*, and we'd managed to survive the first separation, so in my heart it wasn't over. *We're just separating,* I told myself. *We're trying to get back together. And this time I'm determined to make it work.*

Still, it wasn't easy. I didn't enjoy watching Nicole settle into a new place with the two kids, watching her move forward without me. She even found a guy to help out with babysitting and running errands and stuff, someone she'd met skiing in Aspen, and she let him move into the guesthouse, rent free, instead of paying him a salary. His name, as you may recall, was Kato Kaelin.

When that first Valentine's Day rolled around, less than three weeks into the separation, I was in Mexico for a celebrity golf tournament, but I sent Nicole some nice flowers, and a note, and she was very appreciative. I told her I wasn't giving up on us, and I didn't. I was still traveling a great deal, mostly to New York, but whenever I was in town I'd take her out, sometimes alone, and sometimes with the kids.

From time to time we even ended up in bed together. On occasion, she cried after we made love. I don't know if she was crying from being happy or unhappy, to be honest, and I don't think she did, either, but I kept hoping it was because she loved me, and because in her heart she knew that we belonged together.

Still, I wanted to give Nicole her freedom—the freedom she thought she wanted—so I didn't get pushy about wooing her back. It was pretty weird, though. Early on, for example, she went on a couple of dates, and she was a little worried about protocol because she hadn't really dated anyone since she was a teenager. "You think the guy's just trying to get into my pants?" she asked me at one point.

"Honey, what do you expect?" I said "You're gorgeous, you're smart, you've got your own money, and you don't want more kids. For most guys, that's an unbeatable combination."

"So should I go out with him?"

"Yeah. If you like him. Why not?"

"But how do I know if he likes me for me," she said, "and not for something else."

"What? You think he likes you for your car?"

"I'm serious, O.J. This is all new to me."

She sounded like a teenager, but it struck me that in dating terms she really *was* a teenager. "Nicole, stop worrying so much," I said. "You're a great girl. Just be yourself and have fun." I was sitting there, on the phone, trying to build up her self-esteem, and when I got off the phone all I could think was, *Man, that's my wife! That was bizarre!*

If there is one good thing I can say about the separation, it's this: We never fought about anything. In fact, during that entire period we only had one argument, and it was because some of her friends were racking up charges on my account at the golf club in Laguna. My assistant, Cathy Randa, spotted the charges and brought them to my attention, and I immediately called Nicole. "Who the hell do these people think they are, eating and drinking at my expense, and why the hell are you allowing it?" Nicole apologized, promised she'd take care of it, and that was the end of that.

Afterward, we were friendly again—maybe *too* friendly. Nicole got into the habit of calling me two or three times a day, to chat, often about some of the guys she was dating. I thought that was a little strange—I felt she was treating me almost like a girlfriend or something—but I didn't mind. I realized that, if nothing else, I was probably her closest friend, a friend she could talk to about anything, and it gave me hope. She always began by talking about the kids—that was the excuse, anyway—and within a minute or two the conversation shifted to stories about the men in her life. This one guy was a complete schmuck, this other guy seemed so nice at first but had turned into a real creep, and so on and so forth. I would think, *Why are you wasting your time with them? You could still be living with me!* But I didn't say it. I didn't want to push her. I wanted her to know I was there without putting any pressure on her.

Then early in May, while I was back in town for a few days, I was out at a club with a group of friends and ran into Nicole and a couple of her girlfriends. I remember thinking it was kind of odd to see her there: We had been living apart for more than three months, and this was the first time I'd run into her in public. One of her girlfriends made a little joke about the situation: "O.J., are you stalking your estranged wife?" And I smiled and said, "Yeah, me and my whole posse." We exchanged a few more words, everything warm and friendly, then went off to enjoy the club with our respective friends.

Later in the evening, my entourage and I took off for another club, and I guess Nicole was gone by then, because I didn't see her. About an hour later, when I left the second club, alone, I found myself thinking about her, and missing her a little. And on the drive home I decided to stop by her house, the one on Gretna Green, to see if she was still awake. I parked on the street and approached the front door, and as I drew close I noticed lights in the window and went to have a closer look. Nicole was inside, on the couch, with a friend of hers, Keith Zlomsowitch, one of the partners at Mezzaluna, a Brentwood restaurant. It was pretty hot and heavy. I took a deep breath and turned to go, but paused to knock on the front door—I rapped on it twice, hard—just to let them know that they'd been seen.

I went home and got into bed, alone, and I must tell you—I was pretty steamed. I think maybe it was just beginning to dawn on me that the marriage was over, and I wasn't real happy about it.

The next morning, I went off to play golf, and I forgot all my woes, but on my way home I called her and told her that we needed to talk. I stopped by the house and she invited me in, and right away I let her know that it was me who'd rapped on her front door the previous night. "What you do is your business, but the kids were in the house," I said. "I don't think it would be too cool for them to walk in on that shit."

Nicole was very apologetic. She said that she'd been drinking, and that she had never meant for anything to happen with Keith, and that nothing like it had ever happened before.

I didn't know what to say, so I reminded her of our little agreement. "We both decided that if we were going to get involved with somebody else we would tell each other. From where I was standing, that looked pretty involved."

"No," she said. "He's just a friend. It's never been like that with him and that wasn't supposed to happen."

"Well, it happened," I said. "And before it happens again, at least think about the kids."

I left, feeling lousy. In my opinion, shit like that doesn't happen unless you let it happen. You always hear stories about guys crying to their wives about some woman they screwed while they were away on a business trip or something, and how it didn't mean anything—that they'd been drinking and they were just missing them and that *it just sort of happened*. Well, that's bullshit. You've got to be in a place in your relationship for something like that to happen, and I was beginning to see that

Nicole was already in that place. As for me, I wasn't there yet. I was still acting like a married man. And guess what? I hadn't been laid in months.

A couple of weeks later, late that May, my suspicions were confirmed. Nicole went down to Cabo San Lucas with some friends of ours, including Bruce and Chrystie Jenner, and one of them called to let me know that she'd met a guy there. I felt like I'd been kicked in the nuts, but I handled it. Life throws some shit at you, and you deal with it. I went in and looked on my kids. They were both fast asleep. They looked like angels.

A couple of days after that, with Mother's Day looming, Nicole called and told me she was flying back, and wondered if I could drive the kids down to Dana Point so we could all spend the day with her family. I took the kids and met her there, taking flowers for both Nicole and Juditha, and the whole family went to church together. Nicole and I stayed for dinner, and drove back late that night. The kids fell asleep in the car.

"That was nice, Nicole said. "Thanks for coming."

"It was fun," I said. But it wasn't fun. All along, I'd been expecting her to tell me about the guy she'd met in Cabo, per our agreement, but it didn't look like that was going to happen.

We got back to my place and put the kids to bed, and that's when Nicole broke the news. "I met someone," she said. "A guy I'm pretty crazy about."

"Yeah," I said. "I know."

"What do you mean you know?"

"Some of my friends were in Cabo, too, remember?"

I didn't say it angry, and I didn't say it with attitude, and I didn't pass judgment. I just said it: *I know you met someone.* Period.

There was nothing else to say.

When Nicole left, I poured myself a drink and sat on the

couch and tried to figure out what it all meant. Strangely enough, by the time I'd finished my drink I felt kind of relieved. Nicole was telling me it was over. It was that simple. For four months, I'd been wining and dining her and sending her flowers and being the perfect estranged husband, but now I didn't have to keep trying. I had wanted her back, yes, but obviously the feeling wasn't mutual. She was done with me. If I kept chasing her, what kind of fool would I be? Hadn't the woman just told me that she was in love with someone else? So, yeah—I accepted it. My marriage was over. My wife didn't want me anymore. It was time to move on.

2.

—

SO HAPPY TOGETHER

FROM THAT NIGHT on, as God is my witness, I made
absolutely no effort to pursue her—never once talked to her
about the possibility of reconciling—and I defy anyone to show
otherwise. The following day, I called her—and I kept my emotions out of it. "I thought about what you said, and I get it," I
told her. "Let's have the lawyers help us get through this as
quickly and as amicably as possible."

Maybe deep down I hoped she would say something—"Oh
no, O.J.! It's not like that! We can work this out!"—but that
didn't happen. She grumbled a little about the lawyers, but that
was about it, then she started talking about personal shit—
managing the kids' schedules, her crazy family, money issues,
and so on—so I tuned her out. I realized I was going to have to
pull away from her completely, and when she paused for breath
I told her that it might be best if we didn't talk for a while.

"Why?" she said.

"We should let the lawyers handle it," I said.

I'd seen plenty of couples in similar situations, and they tended to get highly emotional during the proceedings, and that generally made everything worse. As I said, I wanted to keep my emotions out of it.

"Okay," she said.

"Great," I said.

I remember hanging up and thinking, *Well, O.J., it's time to get back in the game.*

The funny thing is, during the previous three or four months a lot of my friends—including Marcus Allen and his wife, Kathryn—had been pushing me to start going out with other women, but I wasn't interested. I thought I still had a chance with Nicole, and I thought I should wait it out. I'll be honest with you, I'd been bothered by that one incident—when I saw her through the window of her house, going at it on the couch with Keith Zlomsowitch—but I would have been willing to forget it. The way I saw it—or the way I *rationalized* it, anyway— a fling or two might actually be a good thing, especially if it made her see that I wasn't as bad as all that.

Anyway, it didn't quite work out that way. At the end of the day, we were headed for divorce court, and at that point it was pretty much out of my hands.

That same night, I was out at an L.A. club, with friends, when I ran into a Hawaiian Tropic model I'd known years earlier. She came over to say hi, and to offer her condolences. "I hear you and your wife separated," she said.

"We did more than separate," I said. "We're getting a divorce."

She was sorry to hear that, too, she said, but not so sorry that she refused an invitation to dinner. She came over to the house a few days later, and we had dinner, and all I could think was, *O.J. is coming out tonight!*

Sure enough, after dinner we retired to the bedroom. Just as we were starting to get serious, I heard someone at my front door, so I excused myself and went down to see who it was. Kathryn and Marcus were outside, and they'd brought a friend with them—a woman. Her name was Paula Barbieri, and she was absolutely stunning. I remember thinking that she looked a lot like Julia Roberts, only prettier.

I invited them in and got a round of drinks, and I just couldn't take my eyes off Paula. Unfortunately, she wasn't in the market. She'd gotten married recently, and it hadn't worked out, so she was in the process of getting an annulment. Of course, from where I was sitting, that was a *good* thing.

That's when my housekeeper came into the room and signaled to me. I couldn't understand what she was doing. Couldn't she see I was in the process of falling in love with this gorgeous creature? I got up and went over. "What?" I said.

"There's a woman upstairs, in your bedroom," she said.

Shit! I'd forgotten all about Miss Hawaiian Tropic. I told the housekeeper to have her come down, and she did, and of course Paula and my friends were there, and it was a little awkward. But what could I do? We had another round of drinks, and I showed my guests to the door, and then Miss Hawaiian Tropic and I retired to the bedroom. That was the night I began life anew as a single man.

Of course, the next day, I couldn't stop thinking about Paula, so I called her and we began to see each other, but not romantically. She wasn't ready for that yet—she had that annulment to get through—and I didn't mind. I just felt good being around her: This was the kind of woman a man would wait for. We went out as friends for about a month, and it was a real clean period in my life. I wasn't drinking, and I'd stopped eating meat for a while, and I felt physically pretty good—except for the arthritis, and my knees, which were both banged to hell from the years of football. Paula was also into clean living. She never had anything stronger than a glass of wine, and she was serious about staying in good shape. She had to be: She was a model, and a very successful one at that. Strangely enough, this was the first time in my life I'd been out with a woman who worked. I liked it, to be honest. Maybe it made her more interesting to me, maybe it gave her more substance—I'm not sure—all I know is that every time I saw her I liked her more.

It was during this period that Nicole's phone calls started becoming more and more frequent, even obsessive, you might say. She would begin with some news about the kids, as she always did, then get to talking about her various personal problems—whether it was with friends, with Kato, or even with this guy she was supposed to be so damn crazy about. The constant phone calls got to be a little much, frankly, especially since Paula and I were beginning to get more serious about each other, so most of the time I ignored them. I knew that if it was about the kids, and it was urgent, she'd call Cathy Randa, my assistant, and Cathy always knew where to find me.

Thankfully, I was actually pretty busy during this period. I went down to New Orleans for about ten days, for the Olympic trials, and spent most of July in Barcelona, covering the Olympics. When I got back, I did some traveling for Hertz, and for a few other corporate clients, and in the fall I returned to New York to cover football. I came back to L.A. from time to time, of course—once to do a story on the Los Angeles Raiders, and a couple of times to shoot scenes for the *Naked Gun* sequel—but I hardly ever saw Nicole, and I liked it that way. In fact, whenever I had to pick up my kids, I usually asked Cathy Randa to fetch them for me. I didn't want to get into anything with Nicole—not about the kids, not about her love life, and not about my own love life—and I thought this was the wisest course of action.

Then the calls began again, but this time they were less about her various problems and more about the issue at hand—specifically, the divorce proceedings. This was when she informed me that some of her friends had been advising her to exaggerate my so-called violent tendencies. She had told them what I'd said right after the 1989 fiasco—that I would willingly toss the prenuptial agreement if something like that ever happened again—and apparently they thought she should try to use that to get a better settlement out of me. "They want me to say that I've been traumatized by the repeated batterings," Nicole said.

"*Repeated batterings!*" I said. "What the hell is that supposed to mean? What repeated batterings?"

"I know," Nicole said. "I can't believe it either. They're trying to convince me that I'm a victim of abuse."

I didn't know what she was going to do, frankly, but I figured that when the time came she'd do right by me. As it turned out, I was called to the stand first. I admitted that I'd become physical with Nicole in 1989, and I described in detail the events leading to the blowup, and I pretty much blamed Nicole for the argument. Still, I took full responsibility for my response. I also said that Nicole had attacked me on several occasions, in the years prior and in the years since, but that I had learned to handle it by physically removing myself from the room—from the *house*, if necessary.

Nicole sat in the courtroom, listening, saying nothing, and the session ended before she could take the stand. She came over, smiled pleasantly, and asked if I was free for dinner. We had a very nice time at dinner. I felt like we were married again.

The next day, we were back in court, and it was Nicole's turn to testify, but she didn't show up. She reached me on my cell, in court, and said, "O.J., I just can't do it." I must tell you, I was pretty impressed. She was a good, moral, churchgoing person, and she simply refused to lie.

While we waited for the divorce to become final, we sometimes hung out together, mostly for the sake of the kids, and it was fairly pleasant. There was absolutely no animosity at that point. Some couples get angry and stay angry, and some just feel sad, and we were definitely closer to the latter type. I think, like many people, both of us wished it had worked out. I had always imagined growing old with Nicole, and watching our kids grow up and have kids of their own, but that wasn't in the cards. So I dealt with it—we both did—and tried to get on with this business of living.

My oldest daughter, Arnelle, was in college at the time, and one day she asked me how come I wasn't angry with Nicole. "When she calls, you talk to her. When she asks you for advice, you give it. And when she just needs you to listen to her, you listen. I don't get it. I thought the divorce was her idea."

"What's there to get?" I said. "The marriage ended. We both got us to this place. What sense would it make to be angry with her? When you're angry, you're only hurting yourself. Life is too short to be carrying grudges. You gotta move on."

And that's what we did, Nicole and I—we moved on. I didn't ask about her boyfriends, and she didn't ask about Paula, and whenever we were together we were focused on the kids. The idea was to make them feel safe, to let them know that we were there for them, and that—the divorce notwithstanding—we loved them more than ever.

As it turned out, these little family gatherings began to affect Nicole, too. Before long, she was calling me again, at all hours of the day and night, to tell me how sad and confused she was, and to reminisce about our many years together. I guess that's normal—part of the grieving process or something—but it was beginning to affect my relationship with Paula, and I decided I needed to put an end to it. Now, when the phone rang, I always checked to see who was calling, and whenever it was Nicole I tended not to answer.

One day she kept calling and calling, and I wondered if something was wrong, but I knew Cathy would be picking up the kids later, and dropping them off, and if anything was wrong I'd hear it from her. But about an hour before the kids were due over, they showed up—with Nicole, not Cathy. I hugged and kissed the kids, and they ran past me, into the house, heading for the pool.

"What's up?" I asked Nicole.

"Nothing," she said.

I could see that something was on her mind, but I didn't pry. If she had something to tell me, she'd tell me in due course.

A few days later, when I was in New York, she called. "I need to talk to you," she said.

"Yeah?"

"I'm pregnant."

That kind of threw me a little. "With the guy you're so crazy about?" I asked.

"No," she said. "Someone else."

"So you're not crazy about that other guy anymore?"

"That ended a long time ago."

"Oh," I said. I didn't know what else to say.

"I guess I'm going to have an abortion," she said.

I didn't know what to say to that, either. Was I supposed to give her my blessing or something? "I'm sure you'll do what you think is best," I said.

"Thanks," she said.

"For what?"

"I don't know," she said. "For listening, I guess."

One night, not long after, I was busy in my home office, working, and I could see Nicole was trying to reach me. She called my cell, my home phone, the cell again. I finally picked up, angry. "What?" I barked.

"I want to read you something," she said.

"I don't have time for this, Nicole."

"It's from my will."

I took a deep breath. "Okay," I said. "I'm listening."

"This is in my will, word for word," she said, and she quoted directly from the document: "'O.J., please remember me from early in our relationship, before I became so unhappy and so bitchy. Remember how much I truly love and adore you.'"

"That's very nice," I said.

"Don't forget," she said. "I mean it."

"I won't forget," I said.

"Promise?"

"I promise."

In October of that year, 1992, the divorce became final. Everything had gone pretty smoothly. Finances, custody, visitation—all that stuff that divorced parents are only too familiar with. As part of the custody arrangement, we agreed to spend the first Thanksgiving and Christmas with the kids, as a family, to give them a little more time to get used to the idea that we were no longer together. We figured we'd celebrate Thanksgiving in New York, at my Manhattan apartment, and Christmas in L.A., and Nicole and I discussed every little detail—down to where I was going to get the turkey, what side dishes the kids liked best, and how many pies she thought we would need. Two days before Thanksgiving, with all the travel arrangements in place, she called to tell me that she wasn't bringing the kids to New York.

"What do you mean?" I snapped. "I changed my whole work schedule for this! The network rearranged things so I wouldn't have to go to Detroit so that *I could spend Thanksgiving with my kids!*"

"Well, we're not coming," she repeated.

"Why? You've got to give me a reason!"

"I can't," she said. "Just, you know—the trip's off."

I couldn't believe it. This was the same woman who would call me two and three times a day, to walk down memory lane, to talk about feeling sad and lost, and here she was, telling me she wasn't letting me see my kids over Thanksgiving—and not even bothering to explain herself.

"We decided this in court!" I shouted. "In front of the judge! You can't change the deal on me!"

"I don't like it when you raise your voice to me," she said, and hung up.

I was furious. I called my lawyer and he called her lawyer, but by then it was too late. I didn't get to spend Thanksgiving with my kids, and I ended up going to Detroit for the network, as originally planned, which made *them* happy. Still, I decided I was never going to let anything like that happen to me again, and after Thanksgiving my lawyers called her lawyers and read them the riot act. They agreed to let me have my kids over Christmas, alone, just me and them, and I was immensely relieved and immensely excited. I went shopping for presents, got tickets for shows, and arranged to do all sorts of fun stuff with the kids. It was going to be a nonstop party. I was going to make it a Christmas they'd never forget!

I called my oldest daughter, Arnelle, and asked her to fly the kids to New York, and I booked the three of them on a flight for December 21.

I was excited, but I was still wary—still pissed at Nicole for pulling that little Thanksgiving stunt. Later, I found out that she'd had a fight with yet another guy—the guy that got her pregnant, I think—and that she had been feeling needy and fragile and had wanted the kids to herself. I wondered if she was going to keep her shit together over Christmas, or whether she was going to try to mess up those plans, too. And I wondered whether I was going to get drawn into Nicole's bullshit and drama for the rest of my life. It didn't seem right. I'd always been there for her when she needed me, during the marriage and long after, and I suspected that her inability to get her life in order was going to create endless problems for me and the kids. I didn't like it.

On December 21, I went to the airport to pick up Arnelle and the kids. We were over the moon with happiness. We spent the next day running around town, shopping and eating and having fun and visiting with friends. I thought to myself, *Being a single dad ain't half bad!*

Then the next day, December 23, I got a call from Nicole. She was crying so hard I couldn't understand a word she was saying, but she finally pulled herself together and told me that she desperately wanted to come to New York. "I can't be away from the kids," she said. "I miss them too much. Please, O.J. Let me come. I want to be with my kids. I don't want to be alone."

Now don't get me wrong, I was pissed at Nicole, but I've never been much good at holding grudges. "Okay," I said. "I'll have a ticket for you at the airport."

"Really?"

I guess she couldn't believe it was going to be that easy. "Yes," I said. "I'm sure the kids would love to have you here."

"Thanks, O.J. I mean it."

"There's one catch," I said. "You can't sleep in the apartment with us. Paula wouldn't like it. I'll get you a hotel."

She didn't complain, she didn't say a word, in fact, because she knew this didn't concern her in the least. Paula and I had been dating for several months now, and we were very happy together, and I wasn't going to do anything that might jeopardize the relationship. Of course, Nicole didn't know that Paula wasn't actually going to be there over the holiday—she was spending Christmas in Florida, with her parents—but that didn't make any difference to me. If I let Nicole sleep in the apartment, it would have been disrespectful to Paula, and that wasn't going to happen. Unfortunately, I had to call Paula to tell her what was going on, and I kind of dreaded it. Paula had taken the time and trouble to fix Christmas dinner for me and the kids before getting on her plane to Florida, and this is how I was going to repay her—by spending Christmas with my ex-wife?

"Paula, it's me, O.J. How are things in Florida?"

"Great. How are you? You sound funny?"

"I'm fine."

"How are the kids?"

"They're great," I said. "But I sort of wanted to talk to you about Nicole."

"Nicole?"

"Yeah. She decided she wanted to be with the kids for Christmas. She's flying in tomorrow."

Paula got mad, and things went downhill from there. She hung up on me, and when I called back she wouldn't answer. I called back obsessively, and for a few hours I imagined how Nicole must have felt when she was trying to get hold of me and not succeeding. I left messages— "I'm sorry. I can't do anything about it. She's the mother of my kids"—but Paula didn't return my calls.

Anyway, to make a long story short, Nicole joined me and the kids in New York and we had a very nice time together. We went to Radio City Music Hall for the Christmas pageant, ran around the city like tourists, and on Christmas morning we opened all the presents Santa had left.

That afternoon, the weather was nice, so Nicole and I took the kids for a long walk in Central Park. When we got back, we ate leftovers and put them to bed. Afterwards, Nicole and I packed their bags, for the flight home the next day, and when we were done Nicole poured herself a glass of wine and came into the living room. "Thanks for letting me come," she said. She looked real sad.

"The kids had fun," I said.

"Did you?"

"Sure," I said, trying not to look at her. I didn't know where she was taking the conversation, but I knew I didn't like it.

"What happened to us?" she asked, and she began to cry. "We were so happy together."

"*Us?*" I said. "What do you mean *us?* You left me."

"I'm such a mess," she said, still crying.

"Look," I said, cutting her off. "We had a few great days. Let's not blow it. I have to go to work tomorrow, and I've got notes to review, and the limo's coming at eleven to take you and the kids to the airport."

She finished her wine and left for the hotel, thanking me again, and I went to review my notes for the next day.

At that point, to be honest with you, I really didn't want to hear any more of her shit. Paula was still mad at me—it had taken three days of calling before she even spoke to me—and I was in no mood to listen to Nicole. We'd had some great times together, sure, but the last two years had been torture. Nicole had been erratic, moody, and worse, and it didn't look like she was getting any better. I had vowed keep her at arm's length, and I'd failed, but that Christmas I decided that things were going to change. I was only going to communicate with her if it was about the kids. I didn't want to hear about her personal life. It was *her* life. She had chosen it. She had made that bed, and she needed to start getting used to it.

For the next three months, I hardly talked to her. She called once to tell me that she had decided to get into therapy, and that she was very happy with the shrink she was seeing. This wasn't one of those high-priced, Beverly Hills, you're-a-beautiful-person shrinks, she said—this was the real deal.

"I'm beginning to see that I messed up a lot of things for us," she said. "I'm sorry I blamed you for everything."

"We both fucked up," I said, trying to be generous. "I'm glad you're getting help."

Of course, years later, when I was fighting her family for custody of the kids, my lawyers got hold of some of the therapy notes from her many sessions, and the picture that emerged was a little different. One thing that really pissed me off, and that they tried to use against me, was about the kids, of course. She told her shrink that after that Christmas visit I hadn't called the house in weeks, and she wondered if I even cared how the kids felt about that. It was total bullshit. I *had* called, but I called when Nicole wasn't around, for obvious reasons. On several occasions, in fact, I spoke to Nicole's mother, Juditha, and she put the kids on the line, and I talked to them at length—and my lawyers have the records to prove it. The lawyers also explained, in court, that I had been deliberately avoiding Nicole, whose constant phone calls were beginning to affect my relationship with Paula Barbieri. I had told her, repeatedly, that I didn't want to talk to her unless it was about the kids, and then only if it was an emergency, and I had even made arrangements to have my assistant, Cathy Randa, shuttle them to and from our homes—all because I wanted to avoid further drama.

It worked, too. We went several weeks without a single argument. In fact, the only argument we had during this entire period related to the kids' vacation schedule. I had wanted to take them away for a week in February, and I'd booked a trip in advance, but at the last minute the school told me that it wouldn't be a good time to take them out of class, and they asked me to reconsider. When I called Nicole to try to change the date, telling her I needed to push it back a week, she wouldn't budge. "It's got to be that week or nothing!" she barked. I told her to kiss my ass and hung up.

Later, I found out that she had split with yet another boyfriend, and that she'd been talking to Marcus Allen about it, in great detail, hoping that Marcus would share those details with me. Marcus wasn't sharing anything with me, however, so I was completely in the dark. The other thing she was telling Marcus was that she was missing me, and that she wondered if he thought there was a chance we might get back together. I didn't know about that either, because Marcus wasn't talking, but I never imagined that she was still pining for me. I thought that it was all in the distant past—it was for *me*, anyway—and I was struck by the way the tables had turned. Nicole was the one who had wanted out of the marriage, and I had tried mightily to save it. When it became clear that the marriage was over, however, I found the strength to move on, but Nicole seemed to be having second thoughts about her decision. Now, these many months later, she had apparently come full circle. I didn't know it, of course, but she was looking for a way back.

Late in February, clearly frustrated by my lack of interest in communicating with her, Nicole found another way to reach me: Every time the kids came over, they showed up with home-baked cakes or cookies. "Mom made these for you. They're yummy." I told them to thank their mother, but I opted not to thank her myself. I just didn't want to talk to her. I was done. I had a new woman in my life.

One day, the kids showed up with a CD. "Mom made this for you on her computer," they said. I listened to it and found that every last song was a love song. I was flattered, I guess, and maybe even a little moved, but that didn't change anything. Nicole and I were finished. "Thank your mom for me," I told the kids. But, again, I didn't bother thanking her myself. I didn't want to get into it, because I wasn't going back. And yes, I know this goes against the popular conception—that I was still madly in love with Nicole, and pining to get her back—but it's God's own truth.

One afternoon, I was packing for a trip to Cabo San Lucas, and waiting for my kids to show up. They were going to have dinner at my place, and spend the night, and I was going to drop them back at Nicole's in the morning, on my way to the airport. When I was done packing, I nodded off on the couch, and the phone rang a short time later, waking me. I answered it without checking the caller I.D., and it turned out to be Nicole. "I want to talk," she said.

"I don't want to talk," I said. "It's always a huge hassle. We're not together anymore. I can't be listening to your problems all the time."

"I know, and I'm sorry," she said. "But there's something I need to say to you."

"Okay," I said. "What?"

"I can't tell you on the phone. I need to tell you this in person."

"I can't talk right now," I said. "I have another call coming in." This was a lie, but I wanted to get her off the phone.

"Will you call me back?"

"Sure," I said, but that was a lie, too, and I didn't call her back.

An hour later, my kids showed up at the house, and they had a package for me. I opened the package, which was from Nicole. I found our wedding tape inside, along with a letter. In the letter, which I didn't read till later, Nicole told me that she was learning a great deal about herself in therapy, and that she had come to realize that she was responsible for most of the problems in our marriage. She also said that she still loved me, that she had never stopped loving me, and that she wanted me to know that she believed we'd had a truly great relationship. I had always thought we had a great relationship, so this wasn't exactly a revelation, and as I read between the lines—or not even between the lines, really—it was pretty clear that she was looking for us to reconcile.

I went out to join the kids, and I was surprised to catch sight of Nicole, standing on the far side of the gate, looking toward the house. I didn't know she had dropped the kids off—Cathy Randa was in charge of that—but there she was, staring at me, and it didn't seem right to ignore her. I went over to talk to her.

"So what are you doing here?" I said. "What's with the wedding tape and stuff?"

"I thought you were going to call me back," she said, avoiding the question.

"I fell asleep on the couch."

"Well, like I said on the phone, I have something to tell you."

I was trapped. I sighed a big sigh and said, "Let's take a walk."

We took a little walk around the neighborhood, the same walk we had taken hundreds of times before. It's a nice neighborhood, quiet and peaceful, and we used to love to wander up and down the streets, looking at the houses, chatting with the neighbors. This time we weren't doing much looking or chatting, though—this time she just wanted to talk, and what she wanted to talk about—no surprise—was us getting back together. She repeated she had come a long way in therapy, and that she was sorry about everything, and she was wondering if I could find it in my heart to forgive her. "I've always loved you," she said. "I've never stopped loving you. And I've never told you I didn't love you."

"That's not entirely accurate," I said. "You always told me you loved me, but you said you weren't *in* love with me."

"Well, I was wrong. I'm still in love with you."

"How can you be back in love with me?" I said. "We barely speak anymore, and I've hardly seen you in months."

"I don't know," she said. "I guess I've been dealing with all the stuff I was supposed to deal with, and everything's a little clearer now. I really feel we could make it work."

I couldn't believe this, even though I'd seen it coming. "You're telling me you want to get back together?" I asked.

"Yes."

"I don't think that's in the cards," I said. "I think it might be good for the kids if we tried to have a friendly dinner from time to time, but that's about it."

"You don't have to make your mind up right away," she said. "All I'm doing is putting it out there. All I'm asking is that you think about it."

"I don't understand you," I said. "I'm the same guy you left. I'm the same O.J. I haven't changed a bit."

"Well, I don't want you to change," she said. "You're fine the way you are. I'm telling you *I've* changed."

I thought that was messed up. She was the mother of my children, and part of me still loved her, but I was pretty sure we didn't have a future together. Still, I wanted to let her down easy, so I urged her to focus on the kids. They had always enjoyed spending time with both of us, together, and that had been the original plan when we first separated—to try to keep the kids happy by showing them that we were still a close, loving family—and I thought we could work on that. "I know the kids would love it if we had dinner as a family now and then," I said.

"I agree," she said. "Let's do it."

When we got back to the house, she asked if she could come in. To be honest, I didn't want her to, but it seemed odd to keep her out, what with the talk we'd just had, and with the kids there, watching us standing by the front gate, so I let her in. We got the kids fed and I took them upstairs and put them to bed, and Nicole was still there when I came back down.

"I see you got pictures of Paula all over the house," she said.

"That's right," I said. "In case you hadn't heard, we're dating."

She smiled, trying to hide the hurt, and sat on the couch across from me. I didn't know what she was still doing there, and I was about ten seconds away from getting rude. "Thank you for letting me hang out," she said. "I just didn't feel like being alone."

"That's cool," I said. "But I'm tired, and I've got a plane to catch tomorrow, and I'm going to bed."

"Okay," she said, but she looked disappointed. I walked her to the door and watched her cross to her car. She looked good. She looked as good as she had when I first met her. I thought, *It's amazing the way people can whip themselves into shape when they put their mind to it.*

When I went back inside, I opened the letter and read it. In her letter, Nicole went on at length about the issues we had just talked about—that it was her fault the relationship had fallen apart, and that she had learned through counseling to "turn negatives into positives" and "to get rid of" her anger:

I always knew that what was going on with us was about me—I just wasn't sure why it was about me—so I just blamed you. I'm the one who was controlling. I wanted you to be faithful and be a perfect father. I was not accepting to who you are. Because I didn't like myself anymore.

She told me that after New Year's Eve she sank into a depression and blamed it on what I had called "that 30's thing." She said that she had given up on treating me as if she loved me, but she said:

I never stopped loving you—I stopped liking myself and lost total confidence in any relationship with you.

And she made her goal clear: to have her and the kids move back in with me.

I want to put our family back together! I want our kids to grow up with their parents. I thought I'd be happy raising Sydney & Justin by myself—since we didn't see too much of you anyway. But now, I . . .

I want to be with you! I want to love you and cherish you, and make you smile. I want to wake up with you in the mornings and hold you at night. I want to hug and kiss you everyday. I want us to be the way we used to be. There was no couple like us.

I don't know what I went through . . . I didn't believe you loved me anymore—and I couldn't handle it. But for the past month I've been looking at our wedding tape and our family movies—and I can see that we truly loved each other. A love I've never seen in any of our friends. Please look at the 2 tapes I'm sending over with this letter. Watch them alone & with your phone turned off—they're really fun to watch.

She ended her letter with the following:

O.J. You'll be my one and only "true love." I'm sorry for the pain I've caused you and I'm sorry we let it die. Please let us be a family again, and let me love you—better than I ever have before.

I'll love you forever and always . . .

Me.

At the bottom, she had drawn a smiley face.

I went to bed and reread the letter, and I had trouble falling asleep that night.

In the morning, I woke the kids, got them fed, and dropped them at Nicole's on my way to the airport. I didn't bother going in. I didn't want to see Nicole. The previous day had stirred up a lot of feelings, and I wasn't sure that was a good thing.

On the flight to Mexico, however, I couldn't stop thinking about our conversation, and about the letter. I still had feelings for her, and she was playing to those feelings, and it bothered me. Nicole was the one who had wanted out of the marriage. Why was she coming back now and making things so hard on me?

When I got to Cabo, I stopped thinking about her. A car picked me up and took me to La Palmilla, which was one of the few fancy hotels there—back in those days, anyway—and I unpacked and went off to take care of business. I was meeting with a group of guys who were going to be putting up several hotels and a golf course in Cabo, and they were hoping I'd be able to attract a few high-profile investors. We looked over the plans, talked business, then went off for drinks and dinner.

The next morning, I got a call from L.A. One of my friends, Billy Kehoe, had died unexpectedly, and I was forced to take an early flight back to L.A. I went straight from the airport to a funeral home in Santa Monica, for the wake. The actual funeral was scheduled for the next day, but I wasn't going to make it: I had already made plans to take the kids to Las Vegas the following morning, where we were going to meet up with Paula, and they were so excited that I didn't have the heart to let them down.

Anyway, I got to the funeral home and hung around for a bit, and the first person I ran into was Nicole. She came over and said hi and gave me a little kiss, and she told me she had left the kids at my house. She had been unable to find Kato, she said, and she knew I was taking the kids to Vegas the following day, so it seemed like a good solution.

"How was Cabo?" she asked.

"It was fine. I might build a little house there."

Then we saw Billy's wife and family and went over to express our condolences. Our friendship went all the way back to when Nicole and I were first married, and we talked about the old days, and I could see that stirred up a lot of feelings for Nicole.

When things broke up, Nicole and I found ourselves out in the parking lot, alone. "I'm hungry," I said. "You want to get a bite to eat?"

"Sure," she said.

We went to a little restaurant in Santa Monica, and for some reason Nicole started talking about Marcus Allen and his fiancée, Kathryn, who were about to get married, and who had asked me to host the wedding at my place, on Rockingham. I told Nicole, "It's funny. Kathryn reminds me a little of you when you were preparing for our wedding. She's over at the house almost every day, running around and worrying about every little detail, from the table settings to the flowers to the music. She wants to make sure that everything turns out just right."

Nicole got a sad look in her eyes, and said, "She's a nice girl, that Kathryn."

"She's *more* than nice," I said. "I know you don't know her all that well, but she's been in your corner from the start. When you moved out, and she saw how upset I was, she told me you'd be coming back. 'O.J.,' she said. 'Nicole has been with you since she was eighteen years old. She needs to do this—she needs to find herself—but she'll be back.'"

"That's the same thing I told you," Nicole said. "But when I told you, you didn't believe me."

"About coming back? You never said anything about coming back?"

"No—about finding myself," she said. "I didn't know who I was."

"And you know who you are now?"

"I'm getting closer," she said.

"Well, anyway, let's not go there," I said. "All I was trying to tell you is that you've got a good friend and a big fan in Kathryn."

Suddenly Nicole was crying and I couldn't for the life of me figure out why that would upset her. These big old tears were pouring down her cheeks, and people at the neighboring tables were taking notice. "What's wrong?" I said, whispering. "I wasn't trying to upset you."

"That's not it," she said.

"Then what?"

"Marcus is not your friend," she said.

"What do you mean 'Marcus is not your friend.' What is that supposed to mean?"

She looked at me like she really wanted to say something that she couldn't bring herself to say, and then it hit me. "Did something happen between you and Marcus?" I asked.

She put her head down on the table and started crying louder. I felt like the whole restaurant was looking at us, so I turned and signaled for the check. When I turned back to look at Nicole, she was lifting her head off the table, sniffling, and using the napkin to dry her tears. She looked at me, all pitiful.

"What?" I said.

"Something did happen with Marcus."

Man, I'll tell you, another guy would have probably lost it, but I didn't lose it. I just shook my head, kind of stunned, and the bill came and I paid it and we went outside. I hadn't said a word to her the whole time. I was still trying to process what she'd just told me.

"What?" she said, like she was scared of me or something. "You're not going to talk to me now?"

"I'll talk to you when I can think of something to say."

I drove her back to the funeral home, because her car was still in the parking lot, and I didn't say a word to her the entire time. But when we got there, not ten minutes later, I cut the engine and unloaded on her. "Why did you tell me this shit about you and Marcus?" I said. "I didn't need to know this."

"I just thought you should know," she said, stammering. "He pretends to be your friend, and then he fools around with me. And I don't think it's right that he knows about something that happened between us and you don't."

"Hey, we're not married anymore, remember? You're single and he's single. The only thing I don't get is why you did it. You're always bitching about people cheating and fucking around on each other, and here you are getting it on with a guy who's about to get married."

"I don't know what I was thinking," she said. "He was so nice to me, and he always listened, and it just sort of happened."

"That shit doesn't just happen," I said.

"I'm sorry."

"Forget it. You don't owe me an apology. You don't owe me anything. But I still can't understand why you told me. Or what all you expect me to do. It's not like I'm going to cancel their wedding or something."

"No, of course not."

"You know what I'm going to do?" I said. "I'm not going to do anything. This has nothing to do with me."

"Don't get mad, O.J."

"I'm not mad. I'm just telling you: We're not married anymore, Nicole, and the reason we're not married is because *you* didn't want to be married."

"I'm sorry."

"Stop apologizing," I said. "I'm just telling you how it is."

"So what am I supposed to do about Marcus?"

"See—there you go again! You're asking me what to do. Can't you figure it out for yourself? Isn't that what you wanted? To get out from under my shadow? To go off and be on your own and have your own friends and be your own person?"

She was crying again. "But he keeps calling me."

"So tell him you're going to tell Kathryn."

"You think I should?"

"I bet that would stop him pretty quick."

"I'm sorry," she said again.

I took a deep breath. "You know, Nicole, this right here is why I've been avoiding you. Every time we talk, something comes up. You've got a problem with this or a problem with that, and you put everything on me. 'Help me, O.J.! Fix this for me, O.J.!' Well, I can't be doing that all the time. You asked me to move on, you wanted to break us up, and you got it. We're broken up and I've moved on. Or I'm *trying* to, anyway."

She was crying again. "I'm a mess, O.J."

"You're not a mess."

"Can I come to your house to see the kids?"

"Nicole, come on. They're asleep."

"I want to see them."

"No," I said, but I said it nice. "I'm taking them to Vegas in the morning. You'll see them Sunday."

"Okay," she said, wiping her tears.

She got out of the car and I waited until she was in her own car, then I drove home. The kids were still up, past their regular bedtime, and I got them to brush their teeth and tucked them in. Just as they were falling asleep, someone buzzed my front gate. I went downstairs. It was Nicole.

"What's up?" I said.

"I don't feel like being alone," she said. "I miss the kids."

"They're asleep, Nicole. And I'm tired. I'm going to bed."

"Can I just stay here for a little? Please?"

If you want to know the truth, I felt bad for her. Even with all the therapy and all of these new insights and stuff, it was obvious she was still having trouble getting it together. We went upstairs. The kids were fast asleep. I stripped to my underwear and got into my side of the bed, careful not to wake them. Nicole lay down on the far side of the kids, saying she wouldn't stay long.

I guess I must have nodded off, because the next thing I knew she was standing on my side of the bed, tugging at my arm. A moment later I found myself following her into the bedroom next door, and a moment after that we were making love. It was the first time we'd been together since the split, and I was feeling all sorts of feelings I would have preferred not to feel.

Needless to say, it was all very confusing.

3.

——

PERIOD OF CONFUSION

I WOKE UP EARLY with Nicole still there, fast asleep. I felt pretty bad about the whole thing. I was dating Paula, and I hadn't wanted this to happen, and suddenly I felt like one of those fools that tries to make all sorts of phony excuses for screwing up. I woke Nicole and told her she had to leave before the kids got up—I didn't want them to see her there, and to tell Paula about it—then I walked her downstairs and let her out. I felt lousy. I was cheating on my girlfriend with my ex-wife. How weird was that?

At noon, the kids and I left for the airport and went to Vegas and had a wonderful weekend with Paula. I didn't tell her about Nicole. If that makes me a coward, and I guess it does, then I'm a coward. I justified it like a million guys justify these things: *It was a mistake. It would never happen again.*

When I got back to L.A., Nicole and I got into what I often think of as our Period of Confusion. This was early April, a month before Mother's Day, more than a year before the murders, and

Nicole pretty much began stalking me. She would drive by the house late at night, and if Paula's truck wasn't out front she'd ring the bell. Like a fool, I would let her in. That thing that wasn't supposed to happen again was happening again—two and three times a week. It was messing me up. All the old feelings were coming back, and I kept fighting them, but Nicole was relentless about getting me back. Still, whenever she broached the subject, I would cut her off. "We're not getting back," I said. "We're just doing this."

"Why are we doing this if you don't have feelings for me?"

"I never said I didn't have feelings for this. I said we weren't getting back."

"But—"

"Listen to me: I don't want to talk about it. This is what we're doing and it's all we're doing. There's no future in it."

Sometimes, after we made love, we'd lie there side by side, and Nicole would talk about her therapy. Things were going well, she said, and she was learning a great deal about herself. She got into all sorts of psychobabble about her childhood, and "unfinished business," and about the anger inside her. I listened because she wanted me to listen, and some of it seemed to make sense, but at the end of the day it really wasn't an issue for me. If she believed she was getting better, that was a good thing— and she certainly seemed to believe.

"My therapist says I like to be angry," she said.

"Yeah?"

"She says I look for trouble because it makes me feel alive," she explained. "We've been trying to figure out where this comes from, so we've been talking a lot about my childhood."

"So what have you figured out?"

"Not a lot yet," Nicole said. "This anger thing is mostly unconscious."

It might have been unconscious, but I'd seen plenty of it over the years—especially in the period leading up to the split. Nicole could mix it up with anyone—a bouncer at a club, some asshole at the gym, a close friend—over absolutely nothing. Nicole was always looking to make enemies, and she had finally turned me, the person she was closest to, into Enemy Number One. I was glad she was talking about this stuff with her therapist. I remember thinking that it would have been nice if she'd figured some of this shit out before the marriage fell apart. I didn't say so, though. Instead, I said, "That's good. I'm glad you found a therapist you like."

During this time, this Period of Confusion, we started spending a little more time with the kids, especially when Paula was out of town, which was pretty often. It was actually kind of pleasant, maybe *too* pleasant, and once again Nicole began to drop hints about getting back together. I didn't understand it. She'd gone out to "find herself," as she put it, and all she'd found is that she wanted me back.

I called her mother one day and asked her what was going on. "I'm really confused," I said.

"I'm not," she said. "I never thought Nicole wanted to leave you."

I called her best friend, Cora Fishman, and she told me the same thing. "She loves you, O.J. She was just dealing with her own issues and she let things get out of hand. But I honestly don't think she ever imagined it would lead to divorce."

"I spent months trying to talk her out of it," I said. "She had plenty of opportunities to change her mind."

"She didn't know what she wanted," Cora said. "She was confused."

"Great!" I said. "Now she's not confused and I'm more confused than ever."

"Ron wants to talk to you," she said. "Hold on a minute."

I held on, and Ron, Cora's husband, came on the line. "How you doing, O.J.?" he asked.

"I don't know. Like I told Cora, I'm pretty confused."

"So you've talked with her?"

"With Nicole? Yeah, of course I've talked to her. That's all we've been doing—talking."

"About everything?" he asked, and it sounded like he was fishing.

Then suddenly it hit me. "You mean about Marcus?" I said.

"Wow," he said, taken aback. "She told you about Marcus?"

"Yeah, Ron. She told me about Marcus."

"Good," he said. "Because, you know, I wanted to make sure everything was out in the open. That's the kind of thing where, you know, you find out about it later and it fucks everything up."

"Well it's out in the open, man."

I then called my own mother to tell her what was going on, hoping she might be able to help me shed a little light on the situation. "How do you feel about it?" she asked.

"I honestly don't know how I feel," I said. "When we're together, I see how happy the kids are, and that makes *me* happy, but I don't know that anything has changed. I don't know that *she's* changed."

And my mother said, "O.J., until you figure this thing out, you're not going be able to move forward with your life. You won't be able to commit to a relationship with another woman. You can't go on like this. You have to get clear on your feelings for Nicole."

Paula was away again, on another modeling job, so I called Nicole and asked her if she was free that weekend. This was in late April, 1993. We went to Cabo and had a very nice weekend.

It was just the two of us, with no distractions, and I felt like I was in love with her all over again. When we got back, I was more confused than ever. I was trying to figure out if I was really in love, or if I just loved the fact that she was desperate to get me back. I couldn't help it. If you get dumped by someone, it feels pretty good when they come crawling back. They're telling you that they've screwed up, and that they've loved you all along.

The next day, while I was struggling to make sense of this, she came by to get the kids. They were out back, in the pool. When I went to answer the door, Nicole reached up and gave me a little wifely kiss, then we walked through the house, heading for the pool. She saw the pictures of Paula again, and made a nasty remark, and it really pissed me off. I guess she thought our weekend in Cabo meant I was ready to walk down the aisle with her that very afternoon, and that by this time I should have dumped both Paula and her pictures. "That was uncalled for," I said. "I don't want you here."

"Fine," she said.

She went out back, got the kids out of the pool, and split. I thought, *Great. She made it easy. If I was actually thinking about reconciling—if I was actually crazy enough to think about reconciling—I don't have to think about it anymore.*

Two days later, she called to apologize. She had discussed the incident with her therapist, she said, and her therapist had told her that she'd been completely in the wrong. "We had an amazing weekend, so I was hoping that everything would magically go back to the way it used to be," she explained. "That was a mistake. I'm sorry."

"Fine," I said.

For the next couple of weeks, we kept our distance, but there was no denying I had strong feelings for her. I also had strong feelings for Paula, however, and that relationship was much less volatile, so I wasn't about to make any big changes—my life was good.

Then one morning, a strange thing happened. Paula was in town, and she had spent the night, and we were up early because I was leaving for Cabo that morning. Just as I finished packing, the limo pulled up outside and I looked out the window. The guys I was going to Cabo with were all there. They got out to stretch their legs and looked up at the window and waved.

Paula and I went downstairs and said hello to the guys, then she kissed me goodbye, got into her truck, and drove out the Rockingham gate. Not a minute later, as I was putting my bags in the limo, Nicole pulled up on the Ashford side of the house. The two women had literally just missed each other. I looked over at my friends, and they looked at me, all big-eyed and everything: O.J. *that was too close for comfort!*

Nicole got out of her car and wandered over, smiling a friendly smile. She was wearing golf shoes, click-click clicking down the driveway, and it struck me as pretty funny. Golf had never been her thing, but she'd started taking lessons recently to show me that that she was interested in the same things I was interested in. Nicole gave me an unexpected peck on the cheek, said hi to everyone, and noticed the limo. "It looks like you guys are going out of town," she said.

"We are," I said. "We're going to Cabo to do a little golfing."

"Sounds like fun," she said.

Anyway, the limo was waiting, and we said goodbye and took off, and on the way to the airport the guys ribbed me about that very close call. I remember telling them a little bit about my confused romantic life. I was crazy about Paula, I said, but Nicole had been pursuing me pretty relentlessly lately. "It's making me a little crazy," I said.

One of the guys said, "I wish I had your problems," and everyone laughed.

Anyway, we got to Cabo and hit the links and I forgot all my problems—golf is pretty magical that way—but that evening I got a call from Nicole. She said she was coming to Cabo, too, with her friend Faye Resnick, whom I'd never met, and she told me that she was bringing the kids. The next day, like a good ex-husband, I went to pick my family up at the airport, and I dropped them at this time-share they'd booked. For the next few days, I shuttled back and forth between my friends and my family, enjoying my time on the links, but also enjoying hanging at the beach with the kids, and taking them jet-skiing and stuff. When it was time to head back to L.A., Nicole said, "Why are you leaving? Why don't you stay for a few more days?" And my kids piped in: "Yeah, Dad! Please don't go! We've been having such a great time!" I thought about this—I didn't have all that much to do in L.A., and Paula was away on some modeling gig and wouldn't be back till early the following week—so I decided to hang through the weekend.

It was very nice. For the next few days, we were like a regular family—swimming and playing and eating meals together and just forgetting about the real world.

Faye hung out with us, too. She was dating this guy, Christian Reichardt, a chiropractor, but they were sort of on the outs. From what I overheard during her many phone conversations with him, some of which got pretty heated, Faye seemed to have a little issue with drugs, which she apparently didn't consider a problem. Whenever these calls ended, usually pretty abruptly, Faye would turn to Nicole and tell her that the problem in the relationship wasn't her—it was Christian. I thought that was kind of amusing, because that was pretty much the way Nicole had felt about our relationship. She was perfect, and I was the fuckup. I almost said something about it, but I bit my tongue. We were having a good time and I didn't want to ruin it.

The last night we were there, Faye was back on the phone with Reichardt, crying. Apparently, he was willing to take another shot at making the relationship work, but he wasn't sure he wanted her to move back in with him. Once again, it sounded eerily similar to my own situation. It also made me think about the fact that all relationships are messy, and that everyone suffers through their fair share of pain—and sometimes *more* than their fair share. The more I thought about that, especially given that talk I'd recently had with my mother, the more I began to think that maybe Nicole was right about us. We'd had something special, and if we wanted it badly enough we could have it again. She kept hammering at this during those few days in Cabo: *We were a great couple*, she said. *The kids had never seemed happier. She'd learned a great deal in the sixteen months we'd been apart.*

It finally got to me. This was in May 1993, and that Sunday was Mother's Day. We were still in Cabo, getting ready to fly home the following day, and I finally broke down and told Nicole that I was willing to give the relationship another try. But I made myself clear on one thing. "I can't have you moving back into the house," I said. "That's not going to happen. I'm not going to have the kids move in, then move out again if it doesn't work. They've moved enough, and it's too disruptive— and I'm not going to put them through that kind of trauma again."

Nicole thought this made perfect sense, but she had concerns of her own. "I don't want to be in a position where we have one argument and you tell me it's over," she said.

I thought this was a good point. "Well, okay," I said. "What do you suggest?"

"If we're going to commit to this, we need to commit for a full year."

I thought about that, and it seemed reasonable. It was just one year, but a year that could alter the course of the rest of our lives—hers, mine, and the kids'. "Okay," I said. "You've got a deal."

"No matter what happens, you stick with it?" she asked.

"Yes," I said. "No matter what happens, I stick with it."

"And if it works for a whole year?"

"If it works for a whole year, you'll move back into the house and we'll remarry," I said.

Nicole was so excited that she called her mother, Juditha, and told her what had happened. Juditha asked to talk to me, and I got on the phone and made light of the situation. "I'm not really sure about this little arrangement, but I guess your daughter thinks it's going to work," I said.

Juditha told me she was hopeful, too.

The day after we returned to L.A., Paula got back to town. I called her and told her I had made dinner plans for us, and I went and picked her up and took her to Le Dome, a fancy restaurant in West Hollywood, on Sunset Boulevard. I told her what had happened in Cabo, and I broke the news to her as gently as possible. Paula was not exactly thrilled, as you can imagine. "Don't expect me to be waiting for you," she said.

"The last thing I want to do is hurt you," I said. "But I honestly feel like I've got to give this a try. I'm still very confused about the whole thing, and I need to know if it's going to work. I don't want to spend the rest of my life wondering if I screwed up my whole family. I owe it to myself, and I owe it especially to my kids."

Paula went kind of quiet on me. She was the opposite of Nicole. When Nicole got mad, she got hot and bothered. When Paula got mad, she went cold and quiet.

I drove her home, feeling badly, and she didn't invite me in.

To be honest with you, I didn't know if things were going to work out with Nicole, but in my heart I felt I had to give it an honest shot. In a way, I still loved Nicole, and I wanted the best for our kids.

At first, things went pretty easily. I was in New York for a good part of the summer, working, and when I came home it was always very pleasant, sort of like a family reunion. Sometimes I would spend the night at Nicole's place, on Gretna Green, and sometimes she and the kids would stay with me, on Rockingham. It was a perfect arrangement. I had a family, but I lived alone. How can you beat that?

Before the end of the summer, though, Nicole began putting a little pressure on me about moving back into Rockingham, and I reminded her that we had agreed to try it for a full year before making that commitment. She knew that, of course, but her lease was running out at the end of the year, and she didn't want to move again. It was hard to find a decent rental, she said, and the few places that were available were incredibly expensive. I told her she should consider buying a place. If she ended up moving back into Rockingham, she could treat the new place as an investment, and real estate on the west side of Los Angeles was always a solid investment. It was good advice, but it wasn't what she wanted to hear. She'd go off, pouting, and for a few days I wouldn't hear a word about it. But before long, it began again: "Why can't we just move back in, O.J.? This is silly. You know we're going to be living together soon enough." Whenever she got too pushy about it, I'd basically avoid her until she got the message: *Stop hounding me. We had a deal. Honor the deal.*

It was a pain in the ass, to be honest, and I got tired of the endless bickering, but at least she had enough self-control to keep it from turning into a full-blown argument.

In the fall, we got an enforced break from each other, which was probably a good thing. It was football season, and I went off to do my TV analyst thing with Bob Costas and Mike Ditka. She stayed in L.A., taking care of the kids, and still obsessing about having to move.

She was also spending a lot of time with her friends—people she'd started hanging out with soon after we separated—and I'm not going to beat around the bush: I didn't like them. Period. I wasn't all that crazy about Faye Resnick, who apparently had a little drug problem, I certainly didn't like Keith Zlomsowitch, with whom she'd had her little "accidental" fling, and I wasn't wild about the rest of the gang, either. I had met a few of them around town, mostly recently, when Nicole and I were out and about, and most of them seemed like pretty marginal characters. I thought a few of them lived a little too close to the edge. They seemed to be mixed up in all sorts of shady stuff, and one of them—Brett Cantor, a waiter at Mezzaluna, a restaurant right there in the heart of Brentwood—had been knifed to death earlier that summer. The murder remained unresolved, but there were rumors it was drug-related.

"I don't know what you see in those people," I told Nicole one night.

"They're my friends," she said. "They're nice."

I didn't think that was an accurate description. "I don't want those people around the kids," I said.

"Jesus, O.J.—they're my friends. You make them sound like criminals."

"Maybe they are criminals," I said. "Maybe you should take a closer look."

I kept traveling, generally on business, and when I got home my first priority was always the kids. I was still trying to make things work with Nicole, of course, but there wasn't all that much time for romance, and—to be honest—I'd lost some of my enthusiasm for it. I don't know what it was, exactly. I guess I didn't think it could work, and I didn't like her marginal friends, and I didn't think she'd learned all that much in therapy, to be brutally frank. I was also sick and tired of arguing about our living arrangement. "Let's please don't talk about moving back into Rockingham until we've done our year," I repeated.

"You make it sound like a prison sentence!"

"Nicole, come on. You know what I'm saying."

"My lease is running out in a few months, O.J., and the Rockingham house is empty half the time. I don't understand this."

"We had a deal."

"Can't we change it?"

"Not until we know that things are working out."

"I think things are working out," she said.

"Maybe they are," I said. "But it's early yet."

I was a long way from thinking that things were working out, to tell you the truth. All that talk about therapy and seeing the error of her ways and accepting responsibility was fine, but on closer inspection it seemed like it was mostly talk. I didn't see that Nicole had really changed all that much. She was trying hard—that was obvious—but she was still the same Nicole she'd been when everything started going to hell. She still had that hot temper, and that anger, and that impatience. And she was still blaming me for all her troubles: *You have that big house on Rockingham. I need a place to live. You won't let me and the kids move in.* She was making me the heavy, and I didn't like it. But I'd committed to a full year and I was determined to honor my commitment. The year had begun on Mother's Day 1993, and we were only halfway there.

There were good days, too, though—don't get me wrong. Times when we'd be hanging out with the kids, having fun, or waking up at my place in the morning, just a big happy family—the family we'd always imagined for ourselves. On those days, I actually let myself believe that things were going to work out, and it colored everything. *Life is good. Nicole is terrific. We're going to make it.*

During this period, Nicole's one big beef, which she kept hammering at, mercilessly, was this business about the house: Why wasn't I ready to let her move back in? And my big beef, which I also kept hammering, equally mercilessly, was about her so-called friends—people that definitely rubbed me the wrong way. Those were the two major problem areas, and we bickered about them, sometimes to a point of exhaustion, but we never let the bickering get out of hand. And in fact, whenever things looked like they might blow up, I'd find myself jetting off on business. I'd go to Tampa or Atlanta, say, to interview athletes for the show, or to New York, for my regular network gig, and being away from her and our problems was a real relief.

When I came home, I always appreciated her more, though, because I'd missed her, but within days I felt like I was walking on eggshells. I didn't want to have any more arguments. I didn't want to hear any more shit about our living arrangements. I didn't want to listen to any more stories about her asshole friends.

Luckily, I got cast in the *Naked Gun* sequel, and that kept me busy. We saw less of each other and argued less as a result, and for a while it worked great. Like a lot of people, we got along a hell of a lot better when we were apart, and when we were together we never had quite enough time to get into anything too serious or damaging.

One day, though, on the set of the movie, I ran into a girl who was a stand-in for Anna Nicole Smith, and she and I got to talking. She began to tell me about some of the wild parties she'd been to recently, and how she was always running into Nicole with her little entourage—a group she described as "a pretty rough crowd." And suddenly, I was thinking, *Now that's weird.* This stand-in was basically a part-time hooker—I believe she worked with Heidi Fleiss, the so-called Hollywood Madam—and she and three of her little girlfriends wrote a book about their experiences, *You'll Never Make Love in This Town Again.* Now here she was, a call-girl, telling me that my ex-wife was partying with a "rough crowd." I was pretty upset, as you can imagine, and after the shoot I drove over to Nicole's house and read her the riot act. "I thought I warned you about these people," I said. "I've told you a million times: I didn't want them around the kids."

"They're not around the kids," she said, which turned out to be a lie. "And I don't know what you have against them. They're nice people. They're my friends."

"You better open your eyes, Nicole. Nice people don't go around getting themselves knifed to death. Nice people don't do hard drugs. Nice people don't turn into whores."

"Where are you getting your information?" she snapped.

"I just know, okay?" I said. "I know about the wild parties. I know about Heidi's girls. And I know about these fucking druggies."

"You're crazy."

"This is not what's supposed to be happening in my life, Nicole. We've been back together for five months and you're fucking everything up worse than ever. Why is this shit still going on? What are you doing while I'm in New York and traveling all over the place and busting my ass working? I don't want to hear this bad shit about you, and I don't want to find out you're letting these people near my kids."

I left, still steamed as hell, with Nicole still hollering at me, but I couldn't hear what she was saying, and at that point I didn't really care.

When I got back to Rockingham, the phone was ringing as I came through the door. I looked at the caller I.D. and saw it was Nicole, so I didn't pick up. But she kept calling and I finally had to answer. "What?!" I barked.

"Why did you leave like that?"

"Because I was pissed!"

"You committed to a year, O.J. It's only been five months."

"I know I committed to a year! Who said anything about that?"

"Nobody, but you seemed angry. I didn't want you to be angry."

"How can I not be angry?"

"Please come back here."

"What for?"

"So we can talk about it."

I went back to the house, and to be honest with you I was still angry. I kept going on about these criminals she was hanging around with, and these trashy women, and I told her she had to wise up and look for better friends. I think I kind of worked myself into a frenzy—it was all just pouring out of me—and I guess she got scared or something because she went upstairs and locked herself in the bedroom. I followed her up and banged on the door.

"Let me in!" I said.

"No!"

"You called me to come back here, and now you lock me out?!"

"You're scaring me."

"Just open the fucking door!"

"Stop banging, O.J. Please! You'll wake the kids!"

"Why didn't you think of that before you dragged me back here?! Why did you drag me back here, anyway?! So we could argue about this shit!"

In the middle of this, Kato showed up, so I started venting to him. I didn't realize that Nicole had called the police, and that I was talking so loudly they were able to pick some of it up on the 911 tape. "This goddamn woman!" I told Kato. "She's got drug addicts and hookers hanging around my kids, and I'm pissed about it." I went back and banged on the door again. "Why is this door locked, Nicole?! You asked me to come back here, and I'm here!"

I went back downstairs and kept venting at Kato: "She keeps telling me she wants to make this work, and she keeps telling me she's getting her shit together, but she's a long way from getting her shit together!"

Meanwhile, she made two calls to 911, back to back:

NICOLE: Can you send someone to my house?

DISPATCHER: What's the problem there?

NICOLE: My ex-husband has just broken into my house and he's ranting and raving outside the front yard.

DISPATCHER: Has he been drinking or anything?

NICOLE: No. But he's crazy.

DISPATCHER: And you said he hasn't been drinking?

NICOLE: No.

DISPATCHER: Did he hit you?

NICOLE: No.

DISPATCHER: Do you have a restraining order against him?

NICOLE: No.

DISPATCHER: What's your name?

NICOLE: Nicole Simpson.

DISPATCHER: And your address?

NICOLE: 325 Gretna Green Way.

DISPATCHER: Okay, we'll send the police out.

NICOLE: Thank you.

DISPATCHER: Uh-huh.

I guess at this point she got off the phone for a minute; then she got impatient and called back.

NICOLE: Could you get somebody over here now, to Gretna Green. He's back. Please?

DISPATCHER: What does he look like?

NICOLE: He's O.J Simpson. I think you know his record. Could you just send somebody over here?

DISPATCHER: What is he doing there?

NICOLE: He just drove up again. (Crying.) Could you just send somebody over?

DISPATCHER: Wait a minute. What kind of car is he in?

NICOLE: He's in a white Bronco, but first of all he broke the back door down to get in.

DISPATCHER: Wait a minute. What's your name?

NICOLE: Nicole Simpson.

DISPATCHER: Okay, is he the sportscaster or whatever?

NICOLE: Yeah. Thank you.

DISPATCHER: Wait a minute, we're sending police. What is he doing? Is he threatening you?

NICOLE: He's fucking going nuts. (Crying again.)

DISPATCHER: Has he threatened you in any way or is he just harassing you?

NICOLE: You're going to hear him in a minute. He's about to come in again.

DISPATCHER: Okay, just stay on the line . . .

NICOLE: I don't want to stay on the line. He's going to beat the shit out of me.

DISPATCHER: Wait a minute, just stay on the line so we can know what's going on until the police get there, okay? Okay, Nicole?

NICOLE: Uh-huh.

DISPATCHER: Just a moment. Does he have any weapons?

NICOLE: I don't know. He went home and he came back. The kids are up there sleeping and I don't want anything to happen.

DISPATCHER: Okay, just a moment. Is he on drugs or anything? I need to hear what's going on, all right?

NICOLE: Can you hear him outside?

DISPATCHER: Is he yelling?

NICOLE: Yep.

DISPATCHER: Okay. Has he been drinking?

NICOLE: No.

DISPATCHER: Okay. All units: additional on domestic violence, 325 South Gretna Green Way. The suspect has returned in a white Bronco.

DISPATCHER: Okay, Nicole?

NICOLE: Uh-huh.

DISPATCHER: Is he outdoors?

NICOLE: He's in the backyard.

DISPATCHER: He's in the backyard?

NICOLE: Screaming at my roommate about me and at me.

DISPATCHER: Okay. What is he saying?

NICOLE: Oh, something about some guy I know and hookers and Keith and I started this shit before and . . .

DISPATCHER: Um-hum.

NICOLE: And it's all my fault and "Now what am I going to do, get the police in this" and the whole thing. It's all my fault, I started this before, brother.

DISPATCHER: Okay, has he hit you today or—?

NICOLE: No.

DISPATCHER: Okay, you don't need any paramedics or anything.

NICOLE: Uh-huh.

DISPATCHER: Okay, you just want him to leave?

NICOLE: My door. He broke the whole back door in.

DISPATCHER: And then he left and he came back?

NICOLE: Then he came and he practically knocked my upstairs door down but he pounded on it and he screamed and hollered and I tried to get him out of the bedroom because the kids are sleeping in there.

DISPATCHER: Um-hum. Okay.

NICOLE: And then he wanted somebody's phone number and I gave him my phone book or I put my phone book down to write down the phone number that he wanted and then he took my phone book with all my stuff in it.

DISPATCHER: Okay. So basically you guys have just been arguing?

At this point you can hear me yelling in the background, simultaneously venting to Kato and shouting at her.

DISPATCHER: Is he inside right now?

NICOLE: Yeah.

DISPATCHER: Okay, just a moment.

SIMPSON: Do you understand me? . . . Keith is a nothing.
A skunk, and he still calls me—

DISPATCHER: Is he talking to you?

NICOLE: Yeah.

DISPATCHER: Are you locked in a room or something?

NICOLE: No. He can come right in. I'm not going where
the kids are because the kids—

DISPATCHER: Do you think he's going to hit you?

NICOLE: I don't know.

DISPATCHER: Stay on the line. Don't hang up, okay?

NICOLE: Okay.

DISPATCHER: What is he saying?

NICOLE: What?

DISPATCHER: What is he saying?

NICOLE: What else?

NICOLE: O.J. O.J. The kids are sleeping.

*I guess I'm still yelling at her, still pissed as hell, and Nicole
is sobbing by this time.*

DISPATCHER: He's still yelling at you? Is he upset with
something that you did?

NICOLE: A long time ago (sobbing). It always comes back.
(More yelling.)

DISPATCHER: Is your roommate talking to him?

NICOLE: No, who can talk? Listen to him.

DISPATCHER: I know. Does he have any weapons with him
right now?

NICOLE: No, uh-huh.

DISPATCHER: Okay. Where is he standing?

NICOLE: In the back doorway, in the house.

DISPATCHER: Okay.

SIMPSON: . . . I don't give a fuck anymore . . . That wife of his, she took so much for this shit . . .

NICOLE: Would you just please, O.J., O.J., O.J., O.J., could you please . . . Please leave.

SIMPSON: I'm leaving with my two fucking kids* is when I'm leaving. You ain't got to worry about me anymore.

NICOLE: Please leave. O.J. Please, the kids, the kids . . . Please.

DISPATCHER: Is he leaving?

NICOLE: No.

DISPATCHER: Does he know you're on the phone with police?

NICOLE: No.

DISPATCHER: Okay. Where are the kids at right now?

NICOLE: Up in my room.

DISPATCHER: Can they hear him yelling?

NICOLE: I don't know. The room's the only one that's quiet.

DISPATCHER: Is there someone up there with the kids?

NICOLE: No.

I'm really losing it about here, yelling to beat the band.

DISPATCHER: What is he saying now? Nicole? You still on the line?

NICOLE: Yeah.

DISPATCHER: You think he's still going to hit you?

NICOLE: I don't know. He's going to leave. He just said that . . .

---

* Transcripts of this call show this word as "fists," but I said "kids."

SIMPSON: You're not leaving when I'm gone. Hey! I have to read this shit all week in the *National Enquirer*. Her words exactly. What, who got that, who?

DISPATCHER: Are you the only one in there with him?

NICOLE: Right now, yeah.

DISPATCHER: And he's talking to you?

NICOLE: Yeah, and he's also talking to my—the guy who lives out back is just standing there. He just came home.

DISPATCHER: Is he arguing with him, too?

NICOLE: No. Absolutely not.

DISPATCHER: Oh, okay.

NICOLE: Nobody's arguing.

DISPATCHER: Yeah. Has this happened before or no?

NICOLE: Many times.

DISPATCHER: Okay. The police should be on the way—it just seems like a long time because it's kind of busy in that division right now. (To police:) Regarding Gretna Green Way, the suspect is still there and yelling very loudly. (Back to Nicole:) Is he still arguing? Was someone knocking on your door?

NICOLE: It was him.

DISPATCHER: He was knocking on your door?

NICOLE: There's a locked bedroom and he's wondering why.

NICOLE: Can I get off the phone?

DISPATCHER: You want—you feel safe hanging up?

NICOLE: Well, you're right.

DISPATCHER: You want to wait till the police get there?

NICOLE: Yeah.

DISPATCHER: Nicole?

NICOLE: Um-hmm.

DISPATCHER: Is he still arguing with you?

NICOLE: Um-hum.

DISPATCHER: He's moved a little?

NICOLE: But I'm just ignoring him.

DISPATCHER: Okay. But he doesn't know you're—

NICOLE: It works best.

DISPATCHER: Okay. Are the kids still asleep?

NICOLE: Yes. They're like rocks.

DISPATCHER: What part of the house is he in right now?

NICOLE: Downstairs.

DISPATCHER: Downstairs?

NICOLE: Yes.

DISPATCHER: And you're upstairs?

NICOLE: No, I'm downstairs in the kitchen.

DISPATCHER: Do you see the police, Nicole?

NICOLE: No, but I will go out there right now.

DISPATCHER: Okay, you want to go out there?

NICOLE: Yeah.

DISPATCHER: Okay.

NICOLE: I'm going to hang up.

DISPATCHER: Okay.

Then the cops showed up, two of them, followed by a supervisor, and it took both Nicole and I a little while to calm down. I told the officers that Nicole was exposing my kids to all sorts of unsavory people, which I wasn't happy about, and she told them that all I did was complain about her friends. I don't think they were all that interested in the details, because one cop just cut to the chase: "Has he ever hit you?" he asked her.

"Yeah," she said. "Once. We had this one incident in 1989."

Once. I hit her once—not even *hit* her, technically—and ever since that day I'd been known as a wife-beater. Whatever they were thinking, I wasn't there in the capacity of a so-called wife beater—I was there because I was concerned about my kids.

Let me share with you an excerpt from the civil trial. The man on the stand is Robert Lerner of the L.A.P.D., one of the officers who responded that day, October 25, 1993. The man asking the questions is attorney Robert Baker:

BAKER: Now, in terms of your conversations with O.J. Simpson, Mr. Simpson was upset about the people—and he informed you of this—that his wife was running around with, correct?

LERNER: Correct.

BAKER: And he was upset about the fact that she was, in fact, in his view and from his information, running—having people in the house who were hookers, correct?

LERNER: He was concerned.

BAKER: And he was concerned that there was one person that he thought was bad for his kids and that his wife shouldn't associate with, and he didn't want him around the house; isn't that true?

LERNER. Yes.

BAKER: And that was a gentleman with the first name of Keith, correct?

LERNER: Yes.

BAKER: And he expressed that to you, that in fact these people that were around the house had some sort of dealings with Heidi Fleiss, correct?

LERNER: That's what he indicated.

BAKER: And he was upset about that, those people being around his house where his kids were; he informed you of that, didn't he?

LERNER: Yes.

BAKER: And he also indicated to you, sir, that he never had intended, nor was he ever considering any physical violence to Nicole Brown Simpson that evening, correct?

LERNER. Correct.

BAKER: And he also indicated to you that the door that she said was broken, before that, she told you he broke—it was broken before he ever went to the house. Isn't that correct?

LERNER: That's what he claimed.

This was in October 1993, almost eight months before Nicole was murdered. Still, when the trial finally got underway, everyone acted like my lawyers were making this stuff up. They weren't. Nicole had been associating with hookers and drug dealers and unsavory characters from way back, and I'd been begging her to keep those people away from my children. And I went on record with my concerns that night when I spoke to the police about it.

Now here's the weird part: The next day, the very morning after the fight, I was back on the set, working, when Nicole called. "Hey, how you doing?" she said, as if nothing had happened.

"Fine."

"Did you play golf this morning?"

"No. I'm working. We're shooting."

"So everything's good?" she asked.

She was feeling me out, seeing if I was still angry, and I told her yes, I was very fucking angry. She dragged me back to the house and then called the police on me, and all because I was concerned about my kids, and about the direction her life was taking.

"I'm sorry," she said.

"Great!"

"What are you doing later?"

"Going back to New York. What the hell do you think I'm doing?"

For the next several weeks, I stayed on that crazy back-and-forth schedule. I'd be in New York for the sports show, then fly back late Sunday to work on *Naked Gun* for a couple of days. Then it was back to New York, with a stop or two on the way to interview one athlete or another for the show. Sunday night, the cycle started all over again—like my own personal version of that movie, *Groundhog Day*.

Whenever I was in L.A., visiting with the kids, Nicole was generally on her best behavior, but during this period she began to seem unusually tired. I think the stress of keeping it together around me was almost more than she could take. She really wanted this thing to work, so she was determined to be a good little girl, but the effort left her exhausted. I also began to wonder whether she was doing drugs.

The one thing that she wasn't able to control was this constant harping about our living arrangement. She kept pushing me to let her and the kids move back into Rockingham, and I kept telling her no. I suggested that she rent another place, or, better yet, buy one, and she finally took my advice and found a nice condo on Bundy, near Dorothy Street. There was one major problem, though. She couldn't afford to buy it unless she sold her condo in San Francisco, and because the timing was wrong she was worried about the tax bite. When she looked into it, she discovered that she could avoid that problem by claiming that the place on Bundy was a rental property, and to indicate in her tax return that she and the kids were actually living with me. I didn't want any part of that scheme, and I told her so. "The last thing I need is a problem with the IRS," I said.

"But I don't understand," she said. "I'm going to be moving back in with you anyway."

"I can't do it," I said.

She was pretty angry, and for a while the good Nicole was nowhere in evidence. Luckily I wasn't around too often, but even when I wasn't home she somehow managed to bring her problems to my doorstep—literally. She would come by the house with the kids, say, to use the pool, and she took to ordering Michele around, acting like she still lived there. Michele tolerated it, but there were limits. One day Nicole asked to be let into my home office, which was locked, and Michele told her she'd have to get permission from me. "No one is allowed in Mr. Simpson's office," she reminded her. "It's one of his rules."

"I'm not asking you," Nicole said. "I'm *telling* you."

"I'm sorry, Miss Nicole. I can't let you in without Mr. Simpson's say so."

Nicole went off on her, cursing and calling her names, then went out to the pool and grabbed the kids and took off in a huff. She was making friends left and right.

I came home for Christmas, and we focused on the kids, spoiling them with presents. I got a few small presents of my own, but only one of them really meant anything to me, and that was the fact that we didn't have a single scene or a single argument in the course of that entire week. I don't know if that qualifies as a present, but I appreciated it, and I made a point of telling her so. To be honest with you, when things were good like that, I always found myself feeling badly—always found myself thinking about the way things might have been. Nicole had given me fifteen great years, but that Nicole hadn't been around much recently, and the Nicole who had taken her place was not someone I knew or even *wanted* to know. At that point, I was pretty much biding my time until the year was up. And in some ways, to be honest, I was already gone.

I remember speaking to Nicole's mother about the various problems—the business with the housekeeper, the questionable friends, the drugs—and she was just as concerned as I was. Unlike me, though, she was still hopeful. "Maybe it's just a phase," she said. "Maybe she'll get tired of running around with those people."

"Well, I hope so," I said. "But I don't know. Whenever I try to talk to her about it, she gets pissed off."

"I don't think there's anything either of us can do," she said. "Nicole's going to have to get through this herself."

I wasn't exactly sure what it was she was supposed to get *through*, to be honest. People fail at marriage every day, and they either find their way back or not. The question, for me, even then, was why did we fail—where did we go wrong? Nicole had told me on more than one occasion that she felt as if she'd been with me forever, and that she was tired of living in my shadow. Maybe that was it. Maybe she had sabotaged the marriage so she could go off and relive her lost childhood or something—one of these "delayed adolescence" things. If I was right, and if that was what she had to get through, I figured I had a very long wait ahead of me.

4

THE TWO NICOLES

NICOLE MOVED INTO the Bundy condo in late January and she liked it just fine, but she was still pissed that I hadn't asked her to move back into Rockingham. "I can't believe you made me buy my own place," she whined.

"Nicole, we've been through this. Give it time."

"I'm just saying."

"I know. You've been *saying* for a while."

"Well, it makes me wonder," she said. "I'm trying to be hopeful, but you're making it really hard."

"It's January. We've got four months before Mother's Day. On Mother's Day, it will be exactly one year."

"I know," she snapped. "Stop reminding me. I feel like I'm on trial here."

The move created one other problem for Nicole, aside from the tax issue, and this one concerned her houseboy, Kato. At the Gretna Green place, he'd lived in the guesthouse, but on Bundy all she had was a little maid's room, so she asked me if I'd put him up at one of the three guesthouses on my property. It was supposed to be temporary, until Kato could find a place of his own, and I told Nicole I was glad to help out. Within a week, Kato was living at Rockingham.

Years later, when the trial got underway, somebody floated a crazy story about this. They said that Nicole had offered Kato the maid's room at the Bundy condo, and that he was game, but that I didn't want them living under the same roof. Again, people didn't seem to understand that—by that point—I had absolutely no interest in reconciling with Nicole. After all, if I had wanted her back, she would never have bought the place on Bundy. She and the kids would have moved into Rockingham, which is what she'd been hounding me about all along.

In short order, Nicole began to resent Kato. I don't know what it was exactly, but he was living at the house, and she wasn't, and I think that really pissed her off. I know it makes absolutely no sense, but a lot of the shit we went through made no sense, and I think my theory's as good as any.

Now there were two people at Rockingham that really pissed her off: Michele and Kato. (Three if you count me.) But she kept coming by anyway, mostly to hang out by the pool and to torment me with her unhappiness. At one point, she told me, "O.J., when I come by the house, I don't want to see either Michele or Kato. Kato shouldn't even be on the property, and Michele should hide in her room until I'm gone. You understand? When I'm around, I don't want either of them around."

I looked at her, wondering if she'd lost her mind. Who was she coming by to tell me how to run my home? If she didn't want to see Michele and Kato, she didn't have to come by at all. She could drop the kids off out front, and I'd be glad to hang by the pool with them. I told her as much, and she looked at me with such hatred I thought she was going to leap off her lounge chair and attack me. But she didn't attack me. She picked up her copy of *People* magazine and ignored me.

To make matters worse, several of her close friends started coming by to express concern about the shape she was in, as if I could do something about it. Nicole was still hanging out with that same bad crowd, they said, drinking too much and clearly doing drugs. Every other day, I heard variations on the same tune: "O.J., you gotta do something about it. She needs help."

But what could I do? Whenever I brought it up, which was often, believe me, she told me she didn't want to hear it. Or worse—she stormed out. As usual, everything was my fault. In her mind, if I'd only let her move back into Rockingham, life would be perfect. But I hadn't let her move back in, and all she had was her friends—and a big tax problem. The tax problem was my fault, too, of course. It was *all* my fault. Nicole's life was turning to shit because I didn't love her, and she was certainly lovable, so the problem was me—I was responsible for everything.

One afternoon, she came by the house to drop off the kids so she could run a few errands, and I thought she looked a little glassy-eyed. When the kids were out of earshot, I asked her if she was okay. I did it nicely—not accusing her of anything, not confronting her. "You know," I said, "I'm hearing from a lot of people—your friends mostly—that you're fucking yourself up with drugs and shit. You want to talk about it?"

"*Fucking myself up?* That's crazy? What 'friends' are telling you this?"

"People who are worried about you."

She got mad. She said it was bullshit, that these so-called friends of hers didn't know what they were talking about—that she was in complete control.

To tell you the truth, I didn't have any concrete evidence to back up the allegations. The woman looked worn down, yes, and she was erratic, and sometimes she seemed completely out of it, but it's not like I really *knew* anything. If I had, trust me, I would have done something about it—both for her and for the kids. But when I looked at my kids, and I looked at them closely, believe me, they seemed fine. They didn't look *messed up* or *haunted* or any of that shit. On the contrary, they seemed solid and happy, and they were as loving toward Nicole as they'd ever been, if not more so. If something really bad was going on, I figured I'd see it, but I didn't see a thing—not in them, anyway. In Nicole, though, the changes only became more obvious with time. She became even more erratic, looked even more worn down, and she seemed increasingly lost. It was hard to understand. For as long as I'd known her, Nicole's head and heart had always been in the right place. Whenever any of her friends had a problem, they always went to her first. She was solid and clear thinking, and she always made the right moral decision. But that was another Nicole, and she hadn't been much in evidence lately. In fact, in some ways it was as if the new Nicole was taking over, and I can't say I much liked her.

One day, right around this time, I was just back from New York, sitting by the pool, in a lounge chair, reading, waiting for Nicole to show up with the kids. The moment they showed up, the kids ran off to the guesthouse with a note for Kato. "What was that all about?" I asked her.

"A letter for Kato," she said. "I want him gone."

Kato wasn't home, but the kids left the note there and they obviously knew what it was about: "Kato's a freeloader!" "He's a bum!" "Kato has to find a place of his own because Mom doesn't want him here."

I was shocked, but I bit my tongue until they were in the pool, out of earshot. "Why do you have to go and teach them that shit?" I said. "They're little kids. They don't need to get in the middle of it."

She rolled her eyes and stormed off, disappearing into the house. A few moments later, she was back. "Man, I hate that woman!" She was talking about Michele, of course, and I didn't want trouble, so I went into the house and asked Michele to disappear for a while. "Go down to the Brentwood Mart and get some fresh flowers or something," I suggested. "Nicole will be gone in an hour or two."

Michele looked a little upset, but she knew it was for the best. "Okay, Mr. Simpson," she said, barely audible. "All right. Let me just finish cleaning up the kitchen and I'll go."

I went outside and told Nicole that Michele was leaving for a while, and that she could relax, but she didn't seem very relaxed. She was full of venom. "You've got to fire that woman!" she hissed.

And I said, "Nicole, look, if we get back together, Michele already knows that you and her—it's not going to work out. But let's just wait and see. We're still a few months away from that."

I thought that was a pretty reasonable thing to say, but it must have rubbed Nicole the wrong way. She went back into the house and returned a few minutes later, looking very worked up. "I just hit her!" she said.

"What?!"

"I hit her! I couldn't help it. I hate her attitude!"

"What do you mean you hit her?! You can't hit her!"

I got up from the lounge chair and walked into the kitchen and found Michele sitting there, red-faced, tears streaming down her cheeks, trying to call the cops. "I'm calling the police!" she said. "Look what she did to me! She slapped my face!"

She kept misdialing the number—411 instead of 911—so I went over and apologized for Nicole's behavior and tried to

CONFESSIONS OF THE KILLER

calm her down. "I'll take care of everything," I said, setting the phone back in its cradle. "Please don't call the police."

"You can't just hit a person and get away with it," Michele said, still crying.

"I know, Michele. That's what I told her. I'm sorry. I don't know what's gotten into Nicole lately, but I'll get it handled."

"Well I don't know what's gotten into her, either, Mr. Simpson, but I can't take it anymore."

I went outside, pissed, and confronted Nicole. "How can you do what you just did? How could you hit that poor lady? I don't care if you don't like her attitude—you can't go around hitting people!"

"Don't tell me what to do," Nicole snapped, then got up and went over to the side of the pool and told the kids to get out. "We're going home!" she said. Then she stormed off, with the kids still dripping wet, as if it was me who had done something wrong.

I went back and looked in on Michele again, and I apologized, *again*, and I told her that I was going to get everything handled right away. I then called Cathy Randa, at the office, and she got my lawyer on the phone. I walked them through what had just happened. "You should have let Michele call the police," my lawyer said. "Nothing like an assault charge to teach a person a lesson."

"What am I going to do about Michele?" I asked.

"Talk to her. Make sure she's okay."

When I got off the phone, I went back into the kitchen. Michele had pulled herself together, more or less, but she was still very upset. Before I could ask her if there was anything I could do, she turned to me and said, "Mr. Simpson, I just can't stay here. I'm going to resign."

We went back and forth on this a little bit, but she was pretty

89

determined, so I told her not to worry about finances or anything—that I would take care of her until she was settled and happy at a new job. "Thank you, Mr. Simpson. I promise I won't leave until I help you find someone to take my place."

Within a few days, Michele introduced me to a friend of hers, Gigi, and I hired her on the spot. The very next day—this is in March, 1994—Nicole called to tell me that she thought we should all go to Cabo for a week or two. A bunch of our friends were going, including Bruce Jenner and his wife, Chrystie, and Faye Resnick and her fiancé, Christian Reichardt, and Nicole thought it would be fun. *Fun?* She'd just created all sorts of domestic havoc for me, and now she was talking about fun!

"I can't go," I said, and it was true: I was getting ready to do *Frogmen*, a television pilot, which was going to start shooting the following week in Malibu, and would continue shooting for several more weeks in Puerto Rico. "I've got the show to do."

"That's not till next week," she said.

"I'm not in the mood," I said.

"Honey. Come on. Please. Do it for the kids."

So I went—I'm a pushover—and we had a pretty good time, to be honest. The beach, good food, good drink, jet-skis with the kids, afternoon naps in the shade, and more good food and drink at the end of the day. I had to come back that first Sunday, though, to be on location in Malibu bright and early the next morning, and I left Nicole behind with the kids and our friends.

That Thursday evening, as I was on my way home from the shoot, Nicole reached me on my cell phone. "I'm back," she said.

"I thought you were staying the whole week," I said.

"I missed you. And I know you're going to be in Puerto Rico for a whole month, so I wanted to spend a little time with you before you left."

There was something a little weird about the whole thing—

Nicole was never a good liar, and when we got together that night something told me she wasn't being completely honest with me—but I didn't pursue it. I accepted what she told me and we had a truly terrific weekend together. She was the old Nicole again—the good one.

On Sunday morning, as I was packing for my trip, I suggested hooking up in Miami in two weeks, where one of my friends was getting married. I told her I'd fly up from Puerto Rico, and she could fly down from L.A., and we could have ourselves another perfect weekend. "Just like this last weekend," I said.

"It really was perfect, wasn't it?" she said, and I swear she had tears in her eyes.

"Yes," I said. "It really was."

When I left for the airport, I was in a terrific mood, and I remember calling Nicole's mother from the limo. "I know I wasn't real optimistic about this whole reconciliation thing, but it looks like I was wrong," I said, eating my words. "Things are finally beginning to work out."

"I'm glad to hear it," she said. "I always had hope."

It was a real turning point for me. After months of telling myself that our relationship was going absolutely nowhere, I felt as if we were really going to make it.

When I called Nicole from Puerto Rico the next day, however, she sounded like the *other* Nicole, the one I didn't like. I don't know if it was some kind of drug-induced mood swing or something, but the real Nicole had left the building. I can't explain it any better than that. She just sounded like that other version of herself: Removed, irritable, miserable, venomous—and completely lost.

She was whining about getting older, and how much she hated it, how much it depressed her, and I told her to join the club. I was getting older, too, and a lot faster than she was, but

I dealt with it because that was the only option. I asked her to put the kids on the phone, and chatted with them about their day, then I told them I loved them and to go to bed and to behave themselves.

The next evening, when I called to check in, she was even more venomous than the previous night: "Why are you calling me?" she snapped.

"*Why am I calling you?* To see what's happening. To speak with the kids."

"You're checking up on me, aren't you?"

"Why would I be checking up on you? What have I got to check up on you for?"

"I don't want to talk to you," she said.

"Well, I don't want to talk to you, either!" I said. "Put the kids on the phone."

Man, it was weird! This was not the Nicole I'd known and loved for the better part of seventeen years. This was a whole, 'nother person. At that point, even an idiot could have told you that drugs were involved. You don't get mood swings like that from eating Wheaties.

I called again a couple of days later, to talk about the Miami trip. Don't ask me why, but we'd discussed it and I thought it was still happening. Maybe I was still hopeful. After all, less than a week earlier I'd called her mother to tell her that things were going great, and they *had* been going great—so it seemed a little strange to just give up on her.

"What *about* Miami?" she snapped, that edge in her voice again.

"We've got to figure out the flights and stuff," I said.

"I don't have time for this shit right now. Stop hassling me!"

"*Hassling you?* How the fuck am I hassling you? I'm trying to plan our trip!"

"Well, this isn't the time for it!" she said, and she hung up.

The next morning, early, my phone rang. It was her. "Hi honey. Did you sleep well? Do you have a big day on the set?" Holy shit. What was I dealing with here?

She called again the next day to tell me that she had spoken to her mother, who had agreed to come up the following weekend to take care of the kids while we were in Miami. But at that point I was no longer interested in going to Miami with her. I felt like a goddamn yo-yo.

"What do you mean we're not going?" she said. "Why?"

"It's just too much of a headache," I said. "I'm tired. It's not worth all the flying."

She could see I was bullshitting her, and she knew it was because I'd finally had enough of her crap. "O.J., don't do this," she said, whimpering. "It's not me. It's Faye. She's doing drugs again, and it's really bad this time, and she has me really worried. And Cora and Ron are having trouble. Their marriage looks like it's falling apart."

"What do you mean?" I asked. "Why?"

"I don't know. It's complicated."

I felt bad about Ron and Cora. They were good people, and Cora was a genuinely terrific human being. I didn't feel all that bad about Faye, though. I'd always felt that she'd been a terrible influence on Nicole, and from what I was hearing those influences were only getting worse.

"I'm really stressed out by all of this," Nicole said. "I know I've been a little on edge lately, but it's really not my fault."

That was kind of the last straw for me. Nicole was always blaming other people for her fuck ups. When she had me, it was me. Now that she didn't have me, it was the people closest to her. "We're not going to Miami," I repeated.

"Don't do this to me, O.J. I was really looking forward to it."

"I'm not doing anything to you. I just want to get through this shoot and come home."

"Are you saying this isn't working?"

Christ! What was I supposed to say to that? Wasn't it obvious? "Well," I said. "I'm not feeling all that optimistic. And if you honestly feel it's working, then something is really wrong with this picture."

I guess I was trying to be honest, and maybe I was a little too blunt about it, but maybe she needed that bluntness to get her mind around the situation.

When I got back to L.A., I knew almost immediately that it was over. The other Nicole had won. She came by the house with the kids and immediately got into another argument with Kato, calling him a "useless freeloader" and worse—right in front of the kids. It was scary. Her entire face was transformed by rage.

Later, when she was somewhat calmer, and I was trying to pull the story out of her, trying to figure out what had set her off, she told me that Kato wasn't doing his job. He never helped with the kids anymore, he never ran errands, and he didn't return her calls when she most needed him. "You've got to kick him out," she said. I told her that she should deal with him herself—Kato was her problem, not mine—and I suggested that she should back off a little. "I think he's actually been looking for a place to live," I said.

She looked at me, pissed, shaking her head from side to side. "You don't give a shit what happens to me, do you?"

"You're wrong, Nicole. I do give a shit. But I can't fix everything."

Man, I'll tell you: I was really looking forward to Mother's Day. It was time to bail.

From that day on, I tried hard to keep my distance. The only time I saw her was when I was picking up or dropping off the kids, or on those rare occasions when she herself dropped them at Rockingham. She didn't look good. She looked tired and strung out, and she seemed to be getting progressively worse. She seemed beaten, in fact.

When Mother's Day finally rolled around, I can honestly tell you that I had never looked forward with so much pleasure to *any* Mother's Day in my entire life. A year earlier, also on Mother's Day, we had decided to try to save our marriage, and we had given ourselves a full year to do it. Now the year was drawing to a close.

That weekend, we drove down to Laguna—I had a house there, and the Browns lived nearby, in Dana Point. On Saturday, Nicole and I went out to dinner, and I basically told her it was over. To be honest with you, it wasn't a big deal. She knew as well as I did that it was over, so this was really more of a formality.

"Maybe we tried to get back together too soon," she said.

"What do you mean?"

"That maybe we should have stayed apart longer. I should have worked on myself a little more before asking you to try again."

"Well, you know, now that you mention it, that's my one concern," I said.

"What?"

"You. I want to make sure you're okay."

"I'm fine," she said, and she changed the subject. Suddenly she was talking about Cora Fishman again, and about the complications in her marriage. "I feel kind of bad about it," she said. "Of all the couples we know, Cora and Ron had the best marriage." She also talked a little about Faye Resnick, who was having very serious problems of her own. She was still messing around with drugs, apparently, and her boyfriend had finally read her the riot act. "He's really pissed," Nicole told me. "He thinks Faye is out of control."

"What do you think?" I asked.

"It's not good," she said.

When the food came, we must have looked just like every other married couple in the restaurant. We sat there eating, not saying much, and from time to time I'd reach across the table with my fork and spear something off her plate.

The next day was Sunday, Mother's Day. We went to church with some of Nicole's family. Denise was there with her six-year-old son, and Nicole kept dogging her. "Why is he wearing a black shirt and black pants? What kind of outfit is that for a little boy? And in *church*, no less." Nicole was venomous, full of rage and anger, and I kept my distance for the rest of the day.

By nightfall, the bad mood had passed. We drove back to Los Angeles, to her place on Bundy, and I went inside and helped her put the kids to bed.

"Well," I said, looking at her, and feeling kind of sad. "It's over."

"I know," she said.

We went into her bedroom and made love. We both knew it was going to be the last time, and that this was our way of saying goodbye. It was actually very nice. We fell asleep in each other's arms.

In the morning, before the kids were up, I slipped out of the house and went back to my place on Rockingham.

It was time to get on with my life.

5.

THINGS FALL APART

Later that same morning, I went by the office and told Cathy Randa all about Mother's Day weekend. "We are done," I said. "We are moving on."

"You sure about that?"

"Positive."

Cathy looked sort of relieved, then smiled a big smile and said, "Guess who's coming to town tonight?"

"Who?"

"Paula."

"You're kidding me?" I said.

"No," she said. "She's in New York, on her way to Honolulu, but she's stopping in L.A. for the night. I'm supposed to pick her up at the airport."

"Wait a minute," I said. "Let me pick her up."

"I don't know about that . . ."

"Trust me," I said. "It's definitely over between me and Nicole."

That evening, I showed up at the airport and waited for Paula by the baggage claim. I saw her before she saw me, and she looked as beautiful as ever. She also looked kind of stunned, to be honest. "What are you doing here?" she asked.

"Well, it's been a year," I said. "And it's over."

"You're done?"

"We're done."

I drove her back to her place, and she was shaking her head the whole way, unable to believe that this was really happening. A year earlier she'd warned me that she wasn't the type of girl who would wait around for me, and she hadn't waited around, but suddenly I was there, and she was there, and we both still wanted each other.

We spent the night together, and the next day I took her to the airport. We were happy, like a pair of kids, and I drove home wondering why I'd ever put her through such hell. I was also grateful—she was being incredibly understanding. When I reached her in Honolulu later that day, however, she sounded a little less happy. "I'm still hurt," she said.

"I'm sorry," I said. "I did what I had to do. If I hadn't made an effort to keep the family together, I would have wondered about it for the rest of my life."

"It was a long year," she said.

"It was long for me, too."

"I don't honestly know what I want from you," she said. "All I know is that I want to take it real slow."

I was game for anything, and I told her so. I wanted Paula back in my life and I made it clear that I'd jump through hoops for her. On the other hand, to be completely honest, I wasn't sure we could make it work. Paula was looking to settle down and start making babies, and I was done with that part of my life. I figured we could have that conversation when she returned to Los

Angeles, but it never happened. A few weeks later, Nicole and Ron Goldman were dead, and I was being charged with the murders.

But I'm getting ahead of myself again.

A few days after Paula left for Honolulu, I was in New York on business, and I got a call from Gigi, my housekeeper. She was upset. She said Nicole had just been by the house, and that she'd asked her to take care of the kids that weekend.

"What are you crying about?" I asked. "That's no reason to cry."

"Nicole got mad at me," Gigi said.

"What do you mean she got mad? What right does she have to get mad? You work for me, and you're off on weekends. If you want to babysit the kids, that's between you and Nicole, but she can't be coming by making demands."

"Yes, sir. That's what I tried to tell her, but she said I'd better be here when she came by to drop off the kids."

"That's crazy! She's got no right even *coming* by the house when I'm not there. Don't worry about a thing. I'll take care of it right away."

I called Nicole the moment we got off the phone. I was pissed, but I kept it civilized. "Gigi works for me, and she has the weekends off," I said. "You can't be hasslin' her. You ran Michele off. Please don't do the same with Gigi."

Nicole didn't apologize, but she didn't come by the house that weekend, either. Two days later, however, when I was back, she stopped by to drop off the kids, and I thought I heard her having words with Kato. I looked out the window but couldn't see her, and I couldn't see Kato, either. He was probably running for the hills. I went downstairs as the kids came through the front door, and Nicole was right behind them, walking in like she owned the place. "I thought I told you to get rid of Kato," she barked.

"I don't want to talk about Kato," I said. "Not now, not ever."

"I never want to see him again," she said.

"Nic, come on—back off. The guy told me he found a place, but it fell out."

"Bullshit."

I ignored her. I took the kids out to the pool and we jumped into the water. Nicole watched us for a few minutes, scowling. "I'm leaving," she said.

I looked at her, as if to say, *So fucking what? Leave already.* She got the message. She turned and left.

I hung out with the kids and tried not to think about her, but it was hard. She was clearly deteriorating. Maybe she was upset because we were over. Maybe she was having a hard time facing the future. I didn't know what the hell it was, but it wasn't good. I found myself thinking of that old cliché about divorce: *If you've got kids, you're stuck with that person for the rest of your life.* It was not a pleasant thought.

After the kids got out of the pool, I called Cathy Randa. I told her I thought Nicole was getting worse, and that I didn't want to be around her anymore. It wasn't good for me, I said, and it sure as hell wasn't good for the kids. I asked her to please review the schedule, and to help me arrange all future pick-ups and drop-offs.

"You okay?" Cathy asked me.

"Yeah," I said. "I'm fine. And if we can get Nicole handled, I'll be better than fine."

I went back to New York on business, and returned a few days later, and the next morning—before I was even out of bed—the phone rang. It was Nicole. "I'm sick," she said. "I've got pneumonia. Could you come by and take the kids to school?"

I got dressed and hurried over. She looked like hell. I changed the bed linens and tucked her back into bed and took the kids to school, then I stopped at Fromin's, a Santa Monica deli, to pick up some chicken soup. I took it back to the house and sat with her, watching her eat it. I didn't understand why she was sick. This was mid-May. Who catches pneumonia in mid-May? I just knew this had to be connected to the drugs. "You're not doing anything you're not supposed to be doing, are you?"

"O.J. Please. How many times have I told you: I don't want to talk about this."

The weird part was, she didn't deny it. She has always been a lousy liar, so she just avoided the topic. I wanted her to talk about it, though. So did her mother. So did anyone who cared about her. Hell, Cora Fishman had *begged* her to talk about it. We all wanted her to face this thing so she could begin to do something about it.

"I wished we had tried harder," she said.

"Excuse me?"

"During the year we tried to reconcile. I know we could have done better."

Now this was something *I* didn't want to talk about, so I said nothing. She set down her soup spoon and stared at me. She looked like all the hope had gone out of her. In the course of the previous year, while we were still working at reconciling, there were times when everything seemed to be going completely to hell—but Nicole never stopped hoping. Now that we weren't even trying anymore, however, there was nothing to be hopeful about, and that's what I saw in her eyes: A complete absence of hope.

For the next few days, Nicole was pretty sick. I ended up shuttling the kids to and from school and to and from my house, and Cathy Randa pitched in, but mostly Nicole wanted me to take care of things. I went to the pharmacy to pick up her medicine, and I went back to Fromin's for second and third helpings of chicken soup, and I helped her change the linens a couple more times. Now don't get me wrong: I'm not trying to suggest that I was the perfect ex-husband. All I'm saying is that I was very worried about her, and that I wanted to help her find her way back. No matter what had gone wrong in our lives—and plenty of shit had gone wrong—she was still the mother of my kids. I was stuck with her, but for their sake I *wanted* to be stuck with her. I've said it before and I'll say it again: Nicole was a great mother. Schoolwork. Manners. Appearance. She was all over those kids. The only thing I objected to was when she turned into the *other* Nicole, and that Nicole was still very much around, still lurking, ready to leap out and make more trouble.

Meanwhile, Paula was back in town, and I was trying to keep that romance going. It was strange. Not all that long ago, I'd cheated on my girlfriend with my ex-wife. Now I was cheating again, in a manner of speaking: I was nursing my ex-wife back to health and trying to keep my girlfriend from finding out.

"I still think separating was a good thing," Nicole told me a couple of days later. We were standing in her kitchen at the Bundy place, and I was ladling hot soup into a clean bowl. "I just wish I'd made a little more progress in therapy."

"You don't think the therapy helped?"

"It helped, I guess. But it didn't really change anything. I wanted to get stronger for us, so that we could have a stronger relationship, but that didn't work out too well."

"Well, you know—that shit takes time."

"I already quit therapy," she said. "I didn't think I was making enough progress."

A few days later—this is in late May, less than a month before Nicole's death—I was having a party at my house for the kids and their classmates. It was a little fund-raiser for the school, and this was the third consecutive year I'd played host. I had clowns and magicians and those bouncy things for the little kids, and of course lots of good food for everyone.

The day of the picnic, Kato was on his way out of the house, to meet some friends, and he stopped by the party to say hello. I heard the kids giving him a hard time—they were repeating all the things they'd learned from Nicole: that he was a freeloader and a bum—and I went over and told them to cut it out. I wasn't mean about it, though. I realized they didn't know any better. Nicole had poisoned them with her anger.

To tell you the truth, though, I was a little sick of Kato myself. I'd already told him to find a place of his own, on more than one occasion, and he kept assuring me that he was trying. It's not like he was underfoot or anything, though, so I didn't give it much thought, but that was one of the things that made it hard for me to understand the depth of Nicole's rage: She saw him even less than I did, but the mention of his name could really set her off.

About an hour after Kato left, Nicole showed up in the middle of the picnic. The first words out of her mouth were, "Where's Kato? I sure hope I don't see him."

"He left," I said. I wondered what *she* was doing there, but since she had often co-hosted that little picnic with me, I wasn't going to ask her to leave.

"You feeling better?" I asked.

Instead of answering, she reached up and gave me a little kiss, then she went around saying hello to the parents, most of whom she knew from school. She was acting very friendly, and behaving like the hostess, and even thanking people for coming.

I thought that was pretty strange. Everyone knew we were no longer together. Everyone knew she didn't live there anymore.

I tried not to think about it. I went inside and joined some of the dads, who were watching the NBA playoffs. A few minutes later, Nicole came down and dropped onto the couch next to me and asked me to rub her feet. I rubbed her feet for a few minutes, mostly because I didn't want to get into anything. She was pale and still looked pretty sick. "You okay?" I asked.

"Uh huh," she said. "Just tired."

I stopped rubbing her feet and told her to go upstairs and lie down, and I said I'd stop in later to check on her. She went, and I thought I'd gotten rid of her, but within a few minutes Gigi, my housekeeper, came by to tell me that Nicole was asking for me. I went upstairs, frustrated, and found her lying on my bed.

"What's up?" I asked.

"Why is Kato still here?"

"*Why is Kato still here?* What the hell does that have to do with anything? He's not here now."

"I hate him."

"For Christ's sake, Nicole, you're the one who asked me to put him up."

"I know," she said. "But that was five months ago. He was supposed to work for his rent, and he's not working. He's not doing shit for me. I keep asking you to get rid of him, and you're not getting rid of him."

"Why are we having this conversation now?" I said. "I've got people downstairs."

"We're having this conversation now because I don't want him around anymore. I don't want to see him when I'm here."

I felt like saying, *Nobody asked you to come by*, but I didn't. The whole thing was crazy. Nicole wasn't making any sense on any level.

"I don't like Gigi either," she said suddenly.

"*Gigi?* What has she ever done to you? What is going on with you, Nicole? Are you on something besides antibiotics?"

"Why are you still giving me shit about that?" she snapped.

"Because I'm worried about you," I said.

"Isn't that sweet?" she said, but she had an edge in her voice. Man, I didn't need that shit. I turned around and left the room without another word. To be honest with you, Nicole's behavior was beginning to scare me.

The party wound down without incident, and Nicole went home, also without incident, but the next day I had Paula over, and we were watching a movie on TV, working on our relationship, taking it slow, when the phone rang. It was Nicole. She was screaming so loud that I had to take the phone into the kitchen.

"Why are you trying to steal my friends?!" she shouted.

"*Steal your friends?* What the hell are you talking about?"

"You invited them to the fund-raiser!"

Jesus! I couldn't believe it. She was talking about the sports banquet I was hosting to raise money for Cedar's-Sinai, for children with birth defects. The previous fall, while Nicole and I were still together, or *trying* to be together, I had suggested that she ask some of her friends to join us at our table. I had my doubts about these so-called friends, but Nicole had told me, repeatedly, that I was wrong about them, and I wanted to give her an opportunity to show me I was wrong. She could bring them to the fund-raiser and maybe I'd find out that they were truly the good, decent people she was telling me they were.

After Nicole and I split up, though, definitively this time, I'd asked Paula to come with me to the fund-raiser. I didn't think she would be all that comfortable around Nicole's friends, though, so I had to disinvite them. Ron Fishman and his son, Michael, were still welcome, as was Christian Reichardt, but I didn't want to force Paula to deal with the girls—Cora or Faye or any of those people—because I didn't think it would be fair to her, or even to Nicole, frankly.

When I called Faye to tell her that the plans had changed, and that I didn't think the evening was going to work out, she tried to set me straight. "I thought Christian and I were your friends," she said.

"Well, you are my friends," I said. (What the hell was I going to say?)

And she said, "Then why can't we come?"

I tried to explain it to her, suggesting that it might be hard on Paula, and she told me that that didn't make any sense at all. "O.J., we don't play that game," she said. "We don't take sides. We want to be your friends, and we'd love to meet Paula."

At that point, what could I do? "Fine," I said. "You can come."

So there I was in the kitchen, with Nicole screaming at me about the fund-raiser, demanding an explanation. "I didn't invite Faye!" I hollered back. "Faye invited herself!"

"Liar!" she yelled. "You're a goddamn liar!"

My God! This woman was crazy. One day I was an angel, the best thing that ever happened to her, and the next day I was Satan himself.

I hung up and called Faye's house. Christian Reichardt answered the phone. I told him what was happening, and he put Faye on the phone, and I explained how Nicole had just gone ballistic over the fund-raiser. "Come on, O.J.," she said. "You know what this is about."

"No," I said. "I don't know what this is about!"

"This has nothing to do with the fund-raiser. Nicole still loves you, and she's upset because you're already back with Paula."

"Who cares about that?" I snapped. "It's over between us. I

can be with whoever I want, and so can she. I don't tell her who to go out with and I don't care, and I wish to hell she'd move on already."

"Well, that's the problem," Faye said. "She can't move on. She loves you. It's easy for you to move on because you don't love her, but she's still crazy about you and can't let go."

I didn't want to get into a long, philosophical conversation. "Faye," I said, "I don't have time for this shit. I just need a favor from you. I need you to call Nicole and tell her that you invited yourself to this thing. You just do that one favor for me, okay? And while you're at it, please tell her I don't give a shit who she dates or anything else."

I know that wasn't the nicest thing to say, but I didn't really care at that point. I was sick of dealing with Nicole's crap. And I had Paula in the other room, waiting.

The rest of the evening went pretty well, and that's all I'm going to say about that.

The next day, as I was heading into town in my car, I saw Nicole and Cora jogging through the neighborhood. I didn't stop, but I called Nicole's house—knowing she wouldn't be there to answer the phone—and left a message on her machine: "I hope Faye explained all the fund-raiser bullshit to you yesterday," I said. "If she didn't, you need to talk to her. I purposely did not invite her and Cora because I didn't feel comfortable having them around Paula. That's the truth. Other than that, please *do not call me for anything.* If it's not about the kids, I don't want to hear from you."

That *was* the truth. It was also definitely true that I didn't want to hear from her. And that right there is the reason we weren't talking at the time of her death. Not because I'd threatened her, but because I'd had my goddamn fill of her. She was poisoning me with her anger, and I needed to get away from it.

The next day, not even two weeks before Nicole's death, Cora Fishman called and asked if she could stop by the house. She lived a couple of blocks away, and she came over, and she was crying before she'd even started talking.

"What's wrong?" I said.

"You've got to do something about Nicole," she said. "You've got to get her away from these people."

"Hey—don't you think I've tried?!"

"Then do it by force if you have to," she said. "Run an intervention. But do something. I'm begging you."

"I'm sick of trying."

"You don't understand," she said. "We had a big fight yesterday, after we went jogging. Nicole is one of my best friends. We've never had a fight like that. She just refuses to accept that she's in serious trouble, and in my heart I know something bad is going to happen "

I'll be honest with you: I liked Cora, but I wasn't moved by her tears. "Don't tell me." I said. "Tell her mother. Tell another friend. I'm finished with her."

"O.J. please!"

"Hey," I snapped. "It ain't my problem!"

That was the end of the conversation.

Much later, of course, during the trial, and during those many months behind bars, I often thought back to that moment, and I felt pretty guilty about it. But at the time I was completely done with Nicole, and I was responding as I saw fit. It seemed like no matter how much I tried to do for her, no matter how patient and reasonable I was, my good intentions always came back to bite me in the ass. So I was pretty angry at that point, yeah. I didn't want to see her, I didn't want to hear from her, and I didn't want to deal with any of her shit. I had done the best I could, and it wasn't good enough, and at that point I wanted to put some miles between us.

Cora left the house, unhappy and frustrated, and I didn't talk to her again until after the murders.

Much later, I heard that the problems over on Bundy only seemed to get worse by the day. Faye Resnick had an acrimonious falling out with her fiancé, and supposedly moved into Nicole's house on or around June 3. Then there was some talk about her going into rehab. But apparently she didn't want to go alone, and she kept insisting that Nicole was as messed up as she was. "I'm not going unless Nicole goes!" she kept hollering, even when they were taking her away. "She's in worse shape than me!" Like I said, I don't know if this is entirely accurate, but that was the story, and I certainly believed one part of it—the part about Nicole being as messed up as Faye. I believed it because I'd seen it.

In a strange way, I was actually kind of hoping that Nicole would hit the wall. I figured she wouldn't even begin to think about acknowledging her problems, or getting professional help for them, until she was completely out of options.

A few days later, while I was in New York, I got a call from Gigi, the housekeeper. I had never heard her so upset. "Nicole was just here," she said, and she began to cry. "She was screaming at me and cursing."

"What was she doing there?"

"She came to tell me that her mail would be coming to the house, and that I should put it aside for her."

That's when I found out that she was still trying to con the IRS. She wanted them to think that she had taken the money from the sale of her San Francisco condo and used it to buy the Bundy condo, another investment property. Only it wasn't an investment property; it was her home. I called my lawyer, steaming. "I can't have her coming by the house anymore," I said. "She already cost me one housekeeper, and now she's got the new one crying and on the verge of quitting."

"So tell her," my lawyer said.

"I don't want to *talk* to her," I said.

"Then write her a letter," he suggested.

We wrote it together. I told her I was not going to risk having the IRS come after me because she wanted to play fast and loose with the tax laws. "I don't want your mail coming to my house," I noted, "so please make other arrangements. Do what you've got to do, but don't make me part of it."

Much later, during the trial, the prosecution tried to make it sound as if I'd been threatening her, and that this was my way of punishing her for leaving me. I don't know how they got that from the facts, but it seems like most reporters never let the facts get in the way of a good story. I was simply trying to keep her on the straight and narrow. The gist of it was, "You're not living here, and you're not going to live here, so you need to take care of this. If the IRS comes, I'm going to tell them the truth."

By this point, as you can well imagine, we were pretty much not talking.

On June 11, I took Paula Barbieri to a fund-raiser for a pediatric hospital in Israel. Margalit Sharon, the wife of the Israeli prime minister, was hosting it. When it was over, Paula and I went back to my place and made love. I felt I had really fallen for her, and things seemed to get better by the day.

The following day, June 12, was the day of Sydney's recital. Sydney was doing a little dance thing at her school, with her little classmates, and I was really looking forward to it. Nicole called me late that afternoon to ask me if I was bringing my son, Jason, and to see whether I could get there early to reserve a few seats. I was tied up with stuff, so I told her I probably wouldn't get there till six, when the recital started. I also told her that I was coming alone. I don't know whether she thought I'd be bringing Paula, but I wanted to set her mind at ease, so I volunteered that information. I had decided not to bring Paula out of respect for Nicole and her family, and I'd already talked to Paula about it. Unfortunately, that conversation had not gone well. She had wanted to come, and she didn't see why I had to keep her away from the Browns. "I don't know why it's such a big deal," she said. "They all know about me."

"I just think it's better this way," I said. "It'll be easier on everyone."

Paula didn't agree and she went all cold on me. I knew I was in for a lot of apologizing, and a lot of damage control. But what could I do? I thought I was making the right decision.

When I got to the recital, I saw Nicole and her parents, Juditha and Lou. Nicole was wearing a short skirt that would have looked inappropriate on a 16-year-old. I thought she looked ridiculous, but I didn't say anything. Still, it really made me wonder. What did she see when she looked at herself in the mirror? Was her mind so muddled that she'd lost her grip on reality?

I went over and said hello to everyone, and Nicole pointed at the seat she'd held for me. It was two seats away from hers. The seats in the middle were for the kids, who would be running around throughout the evening. Nicole's sister, Denise, was in the row in front of me. She turned around and smiled a big smile and reached over and gave me a kiss.

Shortly after the evening got underway, I nodded off in my chair. I don't know if you've ever been to one of these things, but they go on forever, and there were probably twenty numbers before Sydney got her turn on stage. When I woke up, startled, they still hadn't made much progress, and I looked around and noticed that a lot of parents were holding nice bouquets. Damn! I had forgotten the flowers. I leaned over and checked the schedule, and there were at least half-a-dozen acts before Sydney hit the stage, so I worked my way down the aisle and hurried into the parking lot. I got into my car and drove into Brentwood and picked up some flowers, and I got back in plenty of time.

We watched Sydney do her number, and clapped louder than everyone else, and then there was a brief intermission. Sydney came over, beaming, and I gave her the flowers. She looked absolutely beautiful. When she went over to talk to her grandparents, I looked up and saw Ron Fishman, Cora's husband. We shook hands and he led me off to one side. "O.J., man, you wouldn't believe what's going on," he said.

"With what?"

"The women. Everybody's mad at everybody. Nicole's not talking to Cora because Cora's upset about the drug use and about the people she's hanging out with. Faye got kicked out of the house by Christian—drugs again—and ended up at Nicole's. Then they did an intervention without even telling Christian, and for some reason he's pissed off about *that*. It's a mess. It's all a *huge* mess."

"I heard a rumor Faye was messin' up," I said.

"I don't know," he said. "All I know is that they took her to rehab, kicking and screaming. She wanted Nicole to go with her. She said, 'If I go, she needs to go, because she's drinking and doing coke worse than I am.' But Nicole wouldn't go."

"I knew this shit was going on," I said. "I tried to do something about it, but Nicole wouldn't even talk about it."

"I know," he said. "Cora told me that she tried to talk to you about it, and that you said you were sick of all the bullshit."

I felt a little twinge of guilt, but it passed. "What's going on with you and Cora?" I asked. "I'm hearing some stuff."

Ron looked pretty crushed for a few moments, but he pulled himself together. "We split up. We've been together for seventeen years, and it's over."

He didn't tell me what had split them up, and I didn't ask. "Wow," I said. "You're right. It's a huge mess."

"Yeah," he said. "And I'm sure we don't know the half of it."

As I worked my way back to my seat, for the second part of the show, a few people came by to say hello, but I was a little distracted. I didn't like what Ron had said—*We don't know the half of it*—because I knew he was right. There was a lot of weird shit happening around Nicole and those girls, and it only seemed to be getting stranger.

As I sat down, I saw Nicole looking at me, like she was wondering what Ron and I had been talking about, but I didn't say a word to her. I didn't want to get into it. At some point, we were going to have to face this thing head on, and I was probably going to need her family's help, but this wasn't the time or the place for it. I was upset enough. If I talked to her now, I knew I'd just get angry.

I was also very tired. I'd been in about four cities in the past week, and I had a late flight to Chicago that night for a get-together with the people at Hertz. I waited for the second half of the show to begin. That's what I was there for, after all. For my kids. I wasn't going to do anything that might ruin things for them.

The second half seemed shorter, or maybe I just nodded off again. When it was over, Sydney came running over, and we had our picture taken together. Then I ran into Judy, who was all smiles. "Where's Nicole?" she said. "Aren't we going to dinner?"

"You guys are going," I said. "I ain't going."

Denise came over and gave me a big kiss, and Lou showed up and shook my hand and said hello. "I'm not going to dinner," I told him. "I've got to stay away from your daughter." I said it with a big smile, though, as if I was horsing around, but deep down I meant it. I did not want to be around Nicole.

Much later, during the trial, this whole evening became a huge issue. For starters, the prosecution tried to suggest that I hadn't been invited to dinner, and that I was upset about it. I didn't need an invitation. It wasn't like that. If I had wanted to go to dinner, I would have gone. But I'm the one who didn't want to go. I didn't have the energy to get into anything with Nicole, and I knew we'd get into it if I was there. The last time we'd talked, prior to our brief conversation earlier in the day, was when she called to scream at me about taking her friends to that fund-raiser. Faye had spoken to her the next day, to set the record straight, but Nicole had never bothered to apologize to me. If I was pissed off about anything, that was it. I was brought up to acknowledge my mistakes and to do something about them. Nicole had once had the same values as me, but I guess they got lost in the shuffle.

So, no. I did not leave the recital "upset and angry," as some people would have you believe. And I didn't think the Browns were *indebted* to me for all the wonderful things I'd done for them over the years, as other people suggested—though God knows I had done an awful lot of wonderful things for them. And I wasn't in the dark mood attributed to me by several people who were at the recital, including Candace Garvey, wife of baseball's Steve Garvey, who got on the stand and told the court that I was "simmering" and looked "spooky." Hell, even Denise testified that I was in a horrible mood. "He looked like he wasn't there," she said. "He looked like he was in space." All of this would have been very damaging, of course, except that there was a guy from Portland at the reception, and he saw me there, mingling with my family, and secretly shot a little video of me to entertain his friends back home. When the trial eventually got underway, he was back in Portland, watching the proceedings on TV, and he heard all sorts of bullshit testimony about my horrible state of mind. He was a little taken aback, to say the least, so he dug up the tape and sent a copy to Los Angeles, and the defense team later played it for the court.

What was I doing on the tape? I was *laughing*. I was *cracking jokes* with Lou. I was talking to Denise, who leaned over and kissed me—for the *second* time that night. And I was horsing around with my kids.

I was also doing my best to stay away from Nicole, admittedly. I wasn't going to go anywhere near that woman. I was sick and tired of her shit. If she wanted to take herself down, that was one thing.

But I wasn't going to let her take me down with her.

6.

THE NIGHT IN QUESTION

I WAS IN A lousy mood after the recital. I was exhausted, and not looking forward to getting on another plane, but most of all I was upset about my brief conversation with Ron Fishman. I didn't like what Ron had said about Nicole and the girls: *We don't know the half of it.* The half I *did* know about was bad enough, but Ron seemed to think it was worse than either of us imagined. I also thought back to my conversation with Cora, Ron's wife, and felt another twinge of guilt. I'd pretty much given up on Nicole, but she was still the mother of my kids. I had to do something; if not for her, for them.

For a few moments, sitting there in my living room, I wondered if I should threaten to fight her for custody. The idea was not to take the kids away from her—I knew that would destroy her—but to shake her up so badly that she'd finally start trying to get her shit together. The girl was an accident waiting to happen.

As I was thinking about this possibility, Kato showed up. He was carrying a towel and a magazine and asked if he could use the Jacuzzi.

"Sure," I said.

"How was the recital?"

"Fine."

"Did you talk to Nicole?"

"I went out of my way to *not* talk to her," I said.

"You look bummed, man. What happened?"

"Nothing," I said. "This shit's endless. You should have seen the skirt she was wearing. She thinks she's still a teenager."

"Can I ask you something?" Kato said. "Why is Nicole so fucking mad at me?"

I didn't want to get into it—all that business about Kato living rent-free without doing anything to earn it—so I told him not to worry. "You know how she is," I said. "She puts her anger and craziness on everyone else."

I noticed the magazine in his hand. It was the current issue of *Playboy*. Kato flipped it open and showed me one of the girls inside. He said he knew her and could introduce me, but I wasn't interested. He went off to get into the Jacuzzi and I found myself thinking about a Raiders cheerleader I'd known some years back. She looked a little like the girl in *Playboy*. I dug up her number and called, and when her machine picked up I left a message. "Hey, it's me, O.J. I wanted to see how you were doing, and to tell you that I'm a free man—a *totally* free man. Call me." I hung up and realized that I really *did* feel kind of free, but the feeling only lasted a few moments. I found myself thinking about Nicole again, and then about Paula. I was pissed at Nicole, and Paula was pissed at me *because of Nicole*. Maybe I should have taken Paula to the reception. I had tried to be respectful of Nicole and the Browns, and once again I got bit in the ass for my efforts.

I went into my home office and started getting some of my things together for the trip. I noticed I only had hundred-dollar bills, and I knew I'd need a few fives for the airport skycaps, so I went out to see if Kato had any change. He was already done with the Jacuzzi, which he'd left running, and I turned it off and went by the guesthouse.

"Kato, man, please try to remember to turn the Jacuzzi off when you get out," I said.

"Did I forget to turn it off?" he asked.

Man, I used to wonder if the guy was all there! "Yeah, Kato. You forgot to turn it off."

"I'm sorry."

I held out a C-note and asked if he could break it, but all he had was twenties. I borrowed one, and told him I'd pay him back. "I need it," I said. "I just realized I haven't eaten anything, and I'm going to run over to McDonald's."

"Can I go with you?" he said.

"Sure," I said. "But hurry up. I'm pressed for time."

We took the Bentley and ordered at the drive-thru window. I ate my burger on the ride back. Kato saved his for later.

I was busy eating, so I didn't talk much, and I found myself thinking back to the recital, and to how cute Sydney had looked up on stage, doing her little dance number. It put me in a dark mood. The last few times I'd called Nicole to try to get the kids, which I often did on the spur of the moment, she had gone out of her way to make it hard for me. She always found some reason not to let me take them. *The kids are tired. They've just eaten. They've had enough excitement for one day.*

I couldn't understand it. She didn't even want me to see my own kids. It seemed like she was making everything as difficult as possible for me. It's true what they say about never really knowing another person. Nicole wasn't even Nicole anymore. She was a complete stranger to me.

I finished the burger and felt lousy. It had gone down wrong.

When we got back to the house, I went inside and started packing, laying some of my things out on the bed. Then I went to the garage to get my golf clubs. There were a few dead balls in the bag, so I set them on the driveway and chipped them into the neighbor's yard. I couldn't seem to stop thinking about Nicole, though. Usually, when I pick up a golf club, the world disappears—that's one of the things I like about the sport—but this time, I couldn't get her out of my head. I remember thinking, *That woman is going to be the death of me.*

It was probably around 9:30 by then. I figured Nicole and the kids and the Browns had finished dinner and gone their separate ways. As I found out later, they'd eaten at Mezzaluna, an Italian place on San Vicente Boulevard, in the heart of Brentwood. Nicole's mother, Judy, had left her glasses at the restaurant, and she'd called Nicole, who called the restaurant, and learned they'd found the glasses. Nicole was told that Ron Goldman was just finishing his shift waiting tables, and that he would be happy to drop them at the Bundy condo when he was done. I knew none of this, of course. None of this had anything to do with my life. Not then, anyway.

I set the golf stuff aside and fished out my cell phone and called Paula from the driveway. Either she wasn't home or she wasn't answering. I think it was the latter. I'd called her several times that day, to apologize for not taking her to the recital, and it looked like she was determined to punish me. Hell, for all I knew, she was already thinking about moving on. If that was actually the case, I had Nicole to thank for it. The lesson here was simple: It doesn't always pay to do the right thing, especially if you're doing it for people who don't give a fuck about you.

Suddenly I felt exhausted. I was getting old. I could hardly walk anymore, and I'd been told recently that I would eventually have to have both knees rebuilt. Plus the arthritis was killing me. I was on medication, but there were days when my hands hurt so much I couldn't pick up a fucking spoon.

I parked my ass on the low wall near the front door, feeling whipped. I was trying to figure out how it had come to this. I'd been somebody once. I'd had my glory days on the playing field, a number of high-paying corporate gigs, many years as a football analyst, and even something of a career as a Hollywood actor. It wasn't over, not by a long shot, but everything seemed more difficult now. It was a little like that business in *Alice in Wonderland*, where she has to run twice as fast to stay in place. But hey, if that's what it took, that's what I'd do. You don't get anywhere in this crazy world unless you fight for it, and I was willing to fight for it. Still, it seemed like every day it took a little more energy, and Nicole was sapping a lot of my goddamn energy.

That got me thinking about family, the *meaning* of family, and specifically about my own family. My mother and father separated when I was about five or six years old, and we four kids—me, my brother, and my two sisters—stayed with my mother. She worked in a San Francisco hospital for thirty years, put food on the table, and kept a clean house. My father stayed in the picture, though. The marriage hadn't worked out, but that didn't turn them into enemies. He was always around, and that was an important lesson for me: When a marriage fails it doesn't give either parent an excuse to disappear. You have to be there for your kids.

The way my parents saw it, life wasn't about them anymore— it was about the four children they'd brought into the world.

And because they felt so strongly about their responsibilities, they made it work. They talked on the phone every day, but it was never about their own shit—it was always about us kids. And whenever there was a problem, they handled it together.

If it was a question of discipline, though, my father took care of it. And when I say he took care of it, I mean *he took care of it*. In those days, there was whuppings, and everyone knew it. You didn't go crying to Child Welfare or any of that shit, because nine out of ten times if you got a whupping you almost certainly deserved it. Hell, I know *I* did.

Then one day when I was sixteen years old, the old man and I had a little falling out. My mother called him to say I'd been disrespectful to my sister, and he came by the house and called me into the living room and asked me to tell him what had happened. I told him, and in my version of the story—which I firmly believed—my sister had done wrong. My father didn't buy it, though. He told me to go to my room, and I knew I was supposed to go in there and wait for him to come in and deliver his whupping. But as I waited, I decided I wasn't going to get a whupping. I didn't deserve it, and there was no reason in hell I was going to let him raise his hand to me. When he came into my room, I told it to him straight. "You're not going to whup me," I said.

"What did you say, boy?"

"You heard me," I said. "You're wrong this time. You try to whup me, I'll kick your ass."

It was pretty tense. I had defied him, and he didn't like it one bit, but he could see that things had changed. I was almost as big as he was by then, and I knew I could take him, and so did he, I guess. He left my room without saying a word to me, angry as hell, and for the next ten years we didn't talk to each other. That's right: *We went ten years without speaking.* He would come over, and hang out, and we even sat at the same

Christmas table together, but we never spoke. And everyone *knew* we didn't speak. It was like family lore: *The boy defied him, and they haven't spoken a word to each other in years.*

A decade later, when I was married to Marguerite, and with my marriage already in trouble, he was at my house in Los Angeles, celebrating Thanksgiving with the family, and I turned to him and said something about some football game. And man, the whole room went silent! It was like I could hear my own heart beating. Everybody was staring at us: *He talked to him. Did you hear that?! O.J. talked to him!*

And my father just answered, like it was the most natural thing in the world, like our decade of silence had never happened, and that was the day we started talking again.

I think on some level I had always blamed him for my parents' marriage not working out, and over the years I had come to see, slowly, that maybe I'd been a little hasty about passing judgment. I had simply assumed he was the bad guy, but I had nothing to back it up. And while he'd been there for me as a father, I guess I was still angry at him, because I wanted what every kid wants: Both parents, together, under one roof.

Now here it was years later, with my own marriage failing, and I began to see that there really were two sides to every story—and that maybe my father wasn't such a bad guy after all. I'm not suggesting I was fully conscious of this, mind you, but I believe that on that Thanksgiving afternoon, with my own marriage in trouble, I began to see that I'd been pretty hard on him—and that, whatever else had happened, he had always been there for us kids. That was an important lesson for me, and that night, sitting on the low wall in front of my house, my stomach rumbling, thinking about all of this, it hit me with a weird kind of clarity: *If you fuck up your marriage, you try not to fuck up your kids.*

I figured Sydney and Justin would be in bed by then, over at the Bundy condo, fast asleep. I hoped so, anyway. I wondered what their mother was doing at that moment, and I wondered what other unpleasant surprises lay in store for me and the kids. For a moment, I thought back to the night I'd surprised her at the Gretna Green house, going at it on the couch with her friend Keith, in the glow of two dozen candles—*while the kids were in the house*. It made my stomach lurch.

Don't get me wrong: Nicole had been a terrific mother—almost obsessive at times—but she'd been screwing up big-time lately.

It's strange. They say people don't change, but I say they're wrong. People change, but it's usually for the worse.

Ron Fishman's words came back to haunt me: *We don't know the half of it,* he'd said. He was right. We didn't know shit. Nicole was on the fast-track to hell, and she seemed determined to take me and the kids with her.

I shut my eyes and told myself to stop thinking about her. I looked at my watch. It was 10:03. I needed a shower, and I had to finish packing. As I got to my feet, an unfamiliar car slowed near my gate, then pulled past and parked a short way down, across the street. The driver got out and waved from the distance, and at first I couldn't tell who it was. When he came closer, I saw it was Charlie. I'd met him some months earlier at a dinner with mutual friends, and I'd seen him again a few weeks ago, when we'd gone clubbing with the same friends. I liked Charlie—he was one of those guys who is always in a good mood, always laughing—and I told him what I tell a lot of people: *Stop by when you're in the neighborhood.*

I guess he took it literally.

Now picture this—and keep in mind, this is hypothetical:

Charlie reached the gate, and the first thing I noticed is that he wasn't smiling.

"O.J., my man—what's up?" he said. It sounded kind of forced.

"What's up with you?" I said. I went over and opened the gate and he stepped through and we shook hands. "What brings you to these parts?"

"Not much. I was out to dinner with some guys, down in Santa Monica. Thought I'd stop by to say hello."

"You've got a strange look on your face, Charlie," I said. "Something bothering you?"

Charlie looked away, avoiding my eyes. "It's nothing, man," he said.

"Come on," I said. "You can tell me."

He looked back at me, struggling with his thoughts. "You're not going to like it," he said finally.

My stomach lurched again and right away I knew. "This is about Nicole, isn't it?"

Charlie nodded.

"What about her?"

"You're not going to like it," he repeated.

"Just tell me," I said, already riled. "Before I get pissed off."

Charlie took a step back, like he thought I might hit him or something. "A couple of these guys at dinner tonight, I guess they didn't know that you and I were friends," he began, tripping over the words. "They started talking about this little trip they took to Cabo a few months back, in March I think it was, and about these girls they partied with."

"Yeah?"

Charlie took a moment. "It was Nicole and her friend Faye," he said.

"I'm listening," I said. I tried to stay calm, but I was fit to explode.

"There was a lot of drugs and a lot of drinking, and apparently things got pretty kinky."

"Why are you fucking telling me this, man?!" I hollered. I turned and had to fight the urge to put my fist through the Bentley's window.

"I'm sorry, man. I thought you'd want to know."

"Well, I don't fucking want to know! I'm sick of hearing this shit!"

"I'm sorry—"

"That is the mother of my children!"

"I know, man. I'm sorry. That's why I told you. I know you two have been through a lot of shit, and I know it can't be easy, and I thought maybe if you talked to her—"

"*Talked to her?!* What the fuck is wrong with you? I've been trying to talk to her for *years*. She won't listen to me. She won't listen to her family. She won't listen to her friends!"

"O.J., man—I'm not the enemy here."

I turned around, fuming, and tried to count to ten. I didn't make it. By the time I got to three I realized that Charlie was right. He wasn't the enemy. *Nicole* was the enemy. I looked at my watch. I had less than an hour before the limo showed up to take me to the airport, just enough time to drive down to Bundy, read her the fucking riot act, and get my ass back to the house.

"Come on," I said, and moved toward my Bronco.

"Where we going?"

"Just come."

Charlie got in. I started the Bronco and the gate whirred to life and I pulled into the street, the tires squealing against the curb.

"Where we going, O.J.?" Charlie repeated.

"We're going to scare the shit out that girl," I said.

"What? *Now?*"

"It never fucking ends. Every time I turn around, it's something new—and none of it's pretty."

"This isn't a good idea, O.J."

"Fuck that. I'm tired of being the understanding ex-husband. I have my kids to think about."

"I'm asking you, man, please turn around."

"Woman's going to be the death of me!" I said. I was seething by this time, and I began to mimic her: "'I want to grow as a person, O.J. I want to find myself. I'm tired of everyone seeing me as O.J. Simpson's wife. I'm tired of living in your shadow.'"

"O.J., *please.*"

"You want to know how crazy it got?" I said, ignoring him. "After the split, after she dumped me, she began calling to tell me about the guys she was dating. 'Oh, O.J.—do you think they like me for me or do they just want to get into my pants?' And you know what I did? I told her to just have fun. I told her she was a great girl and not to worry and to go with her gut. 'Guys'll be lining up around the block for you,' I said. 'You're gorgeous and you're smart. I know you'll pick the right guys.' Is that twisted or what? I would think, *What the fuck are you doing, O.J.?!* And then I would answer my own question: *Well, the sooner she gets this finding-herself shit out of her system, the sooner she'll be back.*"

"That's fucked up, man," Charlie said.

"Tell me about it!" I said. I glanced over at him. He looked scared. "Relax, man," I said. "I'm just going to talk to the girl. And it'll be quick. I'm leaving for Chicago on the red eye."

"I shouldn't have told you," Charlie said.

"No, man. You did the right thing. This is exactly what I needed—something to shake me up. This shit's been eating away at me forever, and it's got to stop. I want to get on with my fucking life. I've got to get this under control."

"You should let the lawyers handle it."

"Fuck the lawyers. You know what divorce lawyers are? They are the scum of the earth. Preying on people at their weakest and most vulnerable. I know. I've given those scumbags a million dollars already!"

"Maybe they owe you, then."

"Fuck them," I said. "I'm going to take care of this myself."

We were at Bundy by then, where it meets San Vicente Boulevard. I jogged left for a few yards and made a quick right to get back on Bundy. We passed the light at Montana and I slowed near Nicole's place. I kept going, though. I took a right on Dorothy and an immediate right into the alley behind her condo, and I pulled a few yards past it and parked on the far left, near a chain-link fence. I cut the engine and looked back toward the condo. It was so quiet it kind of spooked me. I looked at Charlie again. He seemed pretty glum.

"Which one's her place?" he asked.

I pointed it out.

"I don't like this," he said. "Let's go the fuck back to your house."

"You worry too much."

"What if she's with someone?"

"She better not be," I said. "Not with my kids in the house."

I reached into the back seat for my blue wool cap and my gloves. I kept them there for those mornings when it was nippy on the golf course. I slipped into them.

"What the fuck are you doing, man?" Charlie said. "You look like a burglar."

"Good." I said. I reached under the seat for my knife. It was a very nice knife, a limited edition, and I kept it on hand for the

crazies. Los Angeles is *full* of crazies. "Nice, huh?" I said, showing it to Charlie. "Check out that blade."

"Put that shit back," Charlie snapped. "You go in there and
talk to the girl if you have to, but you're not taking a goddamn
knife with you."

He snatched it out of my hand, pissed.

"You've got to learn to relax, Charlie," I said, then I opened
the door, got out of the Bronco, and stole across the alley.

Nicole's condo was one of two units, both of them long and
narrow, mirror images of each other, fused at the middle. They
each had their own entry, on Bundy, and they each had a back
gate, in the alley, but Nicole's back gate was broken. The buzzer
didn't work properly, and the gate opened if you gave it a little
push. I must have told her a million times—"Please get the goddamn gate fixed!"—but the woman never listened. I slipped
past the gate, into the narrow courtyard, and moved toward the
front door, and right away I noticed lights flickering in the windows. I moved past the front door to take a closer look. There
were candles burning inside, and I could hear faint music playing. It was obvious that Nicole was expecting company. I wondered who the fuck it was *this* time. I wondered if maybe Faye
was coming over with some of her boy-toys so that they could
all get wild and dirty *while my kids were sleeping upstairs.*

Just as I was beginning to get seriously steamed, the back
gate squeaked open. A guy came walking through like he
owned the fucking place. He saw me and froze. He was young
and good-looking, with a thick head of black hair, and I tried to
place him, but I'd never seen him before. I didn't even know his
name: Ron Goldman.

"Who the fuck are you?" I said.

"I, uh—I just came by to return a pair of glasses," he replied,
stammering.

CONFESSIONS OF THE KILLER

"Really? A pair of glasses, huh?"

"Yes," he said. He was carrying an envelope. "Judy left them at the restaurant. I'm a waiter at Mezzaluna."

"So it's *Judy*, is it? You're on a first name basis with Judy."

At that moment, the gate behind Goldman squeaked again. Charlie walked into the narrow space. He was carrying the knife. "Everything cool here?" he asked. "I saw this guy walking through the gate, and I just wanted to make sure there wasn't going to be any trouble."

"This motherfucker wants me to believe that he's here dropping off a pair of *Judy's* glasses," I said.

"I am," Goldman said, appearing increasingly nervous. He held up an envelope. "Look for yourself."

"And then what?" I said. "You were going back to the restaurant?"

"No," he said. "My shift's over. I'm just leaving these here and going home."

"You expect me to believe that?"

"I don't expect anything," he said. "I'm telling you the truth."

"You're a fucking liar!" I shouted.

"I'm not. I swear to God."

"She's got candles burning inside. Fucking music playing. Probably a nice bottle of red wine breathing on the counter, waiting for you."

"Not for me," Goldman protested.

"Fuck you, man! You think I'm fucking stupid or something?!"

Suddenly the front door opened. Nicole came outside. She was wearing a slinky little cocktail dress, black, with probably not much on underneath. Her mouth fell open in shock. She looked at me, and she looked at Goldman, and she looked at Charlie, just beyond. Goldman was pretty well trapped. Charlie stood between him and the rear gate, and I was barring his way to the front.

"O.J., what the fuck is going on?"

I turned to look at Nicole. "That's what I want to know," I said.

Kato, the dog, came wandering out of the house. He saw me and wagged his tail, then he saw Goldman and also wagged his tail. I looked at Goldman, steamed, and Charlie moved closer, the knife still in his hand. I think he sensed that things were about to get out of control, because I was very close to losing it.

"I'm listening, motherfucker!" I said to Goldman.

"O.J.!" Nicole hollered. "Leave him the fuck alone! What are you doing here, anyway? I thought you were going to Chicago."

"Fuck you," I said.

"Hey, man," Goldman said. "That's not necessary."

Charlie piped in. "Let's just get the fuck out of here, O.J."

"I asked you a question, motherfucker. What are you doing here? You delivering drugs?"

"Leave him alone, O.J.!" Nicole shouted.

"I hear half you assholes are dealing on the side," I said.

Nicole came at me, swinging. "Get the fuck out of here!" she said. "This is my house and I can do what I want!"

"Not in front of my kids, you can't!"

"Fuck you!"

"No, fuck *you*. I gave you everything you could ask for, and you fucked it all up."

She came at me like a banshee, all arms and legs, flailing, and I ducked and she lost her balance and fell against the stoop. She fell hard on her right side—I could hear the back of her head hitting the ground—and she lay there for a moment, not moving.

"Jesus Christ, O.J., let's get the fuck out of here!" Charlie said, his voice cracking.

I looked over at Goldman, and I was fuming. I guess he thought I was going to hit him, because he got into his little karate stance. "What the fuck is that?" I said. "You think you can take me with your karate shit?" He started circling me, bobbing and weaving, and if I hadn't been so fucking angry I would have laughed in his face.

"O.J., come on!" It was Charlie again, pleading.

Nicole moaned, regaining consciousness. She stirred on the ground and opened her eyes and looked at me, but it didn't seem like anything was registering.

Charlie walked over and planted himself in front of me, blocking my view. "We are fucking *done* here, man—let's go!"

I noticed the knife in Charlie's hand, and in one deft move I removed my right glove and snatched it up. "We're not going anywhere," I said, turning to face Goldman. Goldman was still circling me, bobbing and weaving, but I didn't feel like laughing anymore.

"You think you're tough, motherfucker?" I said.

I could hear Charlie just behind me, saying something, urging me to get the fuck out of there, and at one point he even reached for me and tried to drag me away, but I shook him off, hard, and moved toward Goldman. "Okay, motherfucker!" I said. "Show me how tough you are!"

Then something went horribly wrong, and I know *what* happened, but I can't tell you exactly *how*. I was still standing in Nicole's courtyard, of course, but for a few moments I couldn't remember how I'd gotten there, when I'd arrived, or even why I was there. Then it came back to me, very slowly: The recital— with little Sydney up on stage, dancing her little heart out; me, chipping balls into my neighbor's yard; Paula, angry, not answering her phone; Charlie, stopping by the house to tell me some more ugly shit about Nicole's behavior. Then what? The short, quick drive from Rockingham to the Bundy condo.

And now? Now I was standing in Nicole's courtyard, in the dark, listening to the loud, rhythmic, accelerated beating of my own heart. I put my left hand to my heart and my shirt felt strangely wet. I looked down at myself. For several moments, I couldn't get my mind around what I was seeing. The whole front of me was covered in blood, but it didn't compute. *Is this really blood?* I wondered. *And whose blood is it? Is it mine? Am I hurt?*

I was more confused than ever. *What the hell had happened here?* Then I remembered that Goldman guy coming through the back gate, with Judy's glasses, and I remembered hollering at him, and I remembered how our shouts had brought Nicole to the door . . .

Nicole. Jesus.

I looked down and saw her on the ground in front of me, curled up in a fetal position at the base of the stairs, not moving. Goldman was only a few feet away, slumped against the bars of the fence. He wasn't moving either. Both he and Nicole were lying in giant pools of blood. I had never seen so much blood in my life. It didn't seem real, and none of it computed. *What the fuck happened here? Who had done this? And why? And where the fuck was I when this shit went down?*

It was like part of my life was missing—like there was some weird gap in my existence. But how could that be? I was standing right there. That was *me*, right?

I again looked down at myself, at my blood-soaked clothes, and noticed the knife in my hand. The knife was covered in blood, as were my hand and wrist and half of my right forearm. That didn't compute either. I wondered how I had gotten blood all over my knife, and I again asked myself whose blood it might be, when suddenly it all made perfect sense: This was just a bad dream. A very bad dream. Any moment now, I would wake up, at home, in my own bed, and start going about my day.

Then I heard a sound behind me and turned, startled. Charlie was standing in the shadows, a few feet away, his mouth hanging open, his breathing short and ragged. He was looking beyond me, at the bodies.

"Charlie?" I called out. He didn't answer. "Charlie?" Still nothing.

I went over and stood in front of him and asked him the same question I'd just asked myself. "Charlie, what the fuck happened here?"

He looked up and met my eyes, but for several moments it was as if he didn't really see me. "Are you listening to me?" I said. "I asked you what happened here."

Charlie shook his head from side to side, his mouth still hanging open, his breathing still short, ragged, and in a voice that was no more than a frightened whisper, said, "Jesus Christ, O.J.—what have you done?"

"*Me?*"

What the hell was he talking about? I hadn't done anything.

I jumped at a sound behind me—a high-pitched, almost human wail. It was Kato, the dog, circling Nicole's body, his big paws leaving prints in the wet blood. He lifted his snout and let out another wail, and it sent chills up and down my spine. "Let's get the fuck out of here," I said.

I hurried toward the rear gate, and moved through it, with Charlie close behind, but I stopped myself before I crossed into the alley. Charlie bumped into me and jumped back, startled. "What?" he said.

I didn't answer. I was thinking about the shape I was in—

I was thinking of all the *blood*. My shirt and pants were sticking to my skin. Even my shoes were covered in blood.

I turned and looked behind me, beyond Charlie, and saw a track of bloody, telltale prints. "I've got to get rid of these fucking clothes," I said.

Without even thinking about it, I kicked off my shoes and began to strip. I took off my pants and shirt, dropped the knife and shoes into the center of the pile, and wrapped the whole thing into a tight bundle. I left my socks on, though. I don't know why, but I didn't see any blood on them, so I had no reason to remove them. As I stood, with the bundle grasped in my left hand, I realized that I'd left my keys and my wallet in my pants. I fell to a crouch and dug for them and noticed that my hands were shaking.

Charlie stood there all the while, mumbling. "Jesus Christ, O.J. Jesus Christ." He just kept repeating himself, like he'd lost his goddamn mind or something.

"Will you shut the fuck up?!" I snapped. I found my keys and my wallet, and rewrapped the bundle, then I stood and hurried across the dark alley. Charlie followed, still mumbling. I got behind the wheel and Charlie climbed into the passenger seat. "Jesus Christ, O.J." he said. "Jesus Christ."

"WILL YOU SHUT THE FUCK UP!"

Charlie recoiled, startled, and shut up. I started the Bronco and pulled out, the tires squealing, and raced through the curved alley toward Montana Avenue. When I reached the end of the alley, I made a left onto Montana and an immediate right at the corner, onto Gretna Green. San Vicente was a block away, and I made a left there and took it all the way to Bristol, then hung a right to Sunset and made a left there, toward home.

I glanced at Charlie. He was hunched over, his elbows on his knees, his face buried in his hands.

"What happened back there, Charlie?" I said.

Charlie sat up. His cheeks were wet with tears. He shook his head from side to side and shrugged.

I thought back to that horrific scene at the courtyard, and to all the blood. I had never seen so much blood in my life. It didn't seem possible. It didn't seem real.

"Charlie?"

He still didn't answer, but what the hell—this wasn't really happening. That hadn't been me back there. I'd imagined the whole thing. I was imagining it *then*. In actual fact I was home in bed, asleep, having one of those crazy crime-of-passion dreams, but I was going to wake up any second now. Yeah—that was it!

Only I didn't wake up.

We were still on Sunset, and I passed the light on Burlingame and made a sharp right onto Rockingham, tearing up the winding hill, toward the house. As I approached the gate, I saw a limo moving toward the Rockingham gate, from Ashford Street, and remembered that I had a flight to catch.

I drove past my house, and past the moving limo, and in the side-view mirror I saw its taillights flare as it pulled to a stop in front of my gate. The driver had probably been waiting on Ashford, out of sight, and I wondered if he'd already called the house. I had no idea what time it was. I looked down at the Bronco's clock and saw it was 10:37. Fuck! I was supposed to be in that limo in eight minutes.

I pulled into Ashford and kept going, hanging a right on Bristol, and I parked in the shadows beyond the home of Eric Watts. There was another neighbor on Rockingham who was closer, but his property ran parallel to mine, and I couldn't get inside without running the risk of being spotted by the limo driver. I was going to have to steal onto my property through the Watts' place, and I knew just how to do it.

I looked down at my lap, at the bloody bundle, then over at Charlie. "You're going to have to help me out here, man," I said.

Charlie turned to look at me. His mouth was hanging open a bit, and he was breathing kind of funny, and he couldn't stop shaking his head. It looked like he was slipping into shock or something.

"Charlie, are you listening to me?"

He stopped shaking his head for a moment, and nodded once, and I began to tell him what I needed from him. "I've got to get into my house," I said. "You're going to have to wait here until I'm in the limo, understand? When the limo's gone—"

Charlie looked away, into the darkness beyond his own window, clearly not listening to me. I reached over and slammed his left shoulder into his seat, hard, and he whipped around to face me, more frightened than ever.

"I need you to fucking listen to me, man!" I shouted. "Are you fucking listening to me?"

Charlie nodded. He looked scared to death.

"Say it! Tell me you're listening."

"I'm listening," he mumbled.

"Let me spell it out for you, and you better fucking pay attention. Are you paying attention?"

Charlie nodded.

"Say it, goddamn it!"

"I'm—I'm paying attention," Charlie said.

"I'm going to sneak back into my house. I'm going to take a shower, and get dressed, and grab my bags, and I'm going to get into that goddamn limo we just passed. Did you see the limo?"

"No," Charlie said.

"Well, there's a fucking limo parked in front of the Rockingham gate, and I'm supposed to be in it, on my way to the airport."

"A limo," Charlie repeated. His mouth was still hanging open, and I wasn't sure any of this was really registering, but I didn't have a choice.

"Once I'm in that limo, and it's gone, I need you to park the fucking Bronco in the driveway, then get into your car and take the fuck off. Do you understand?"

Charlie nodded.

"This here's the clicker. It'll open the gate. You can drop the key in the mailbox, but run out before the gate closes. Okay?"

"Okay," he said.

I took the key out of the ignition and removed all the keys except the one for the Bronco.

Then I set the bundle in his lap. "I need you to take this, and get rid of it," I said. Charlie looked down at the bundle, afraid to touch it. "I don't give a fuck how you get rid of it, but make sure it disappears. You hear? It needs to disappear forever."

Charlie nodded.

"Did you fucking hear me?!" I hollered.

"I heard you," Charlie said.

I made him repeat everything I had told him, word for word, then I got out of the car and stole into the neighbor's property, toward my house. My heart was beating like crazy. I could feel it pounding in my ears.

I moved past the tennis court to the little secret path that connected our two properties. Only a few friends knew about that path, and all of them were tennis players. They made use of it whenever I wasn't around to open the front gate for them.

Within seconds, I was on my property, moving past my own tennis court. I hung left, moving past the guesthouses, all of which are tucked away, out of sight, and past the pool, toward the rear of the main house. I couldn't see the limo from way back there, but I knew it was at the Rockingham gate. I was sure the driver had already buzzed the house by then, and I was pretty sure he'd already called his office to tell them I wasn't there. Still, he was a few minutes early, and he'd hang tight. He'd buzz again in a few minutes. For all I knew, he was buzzing at that very moment.

As I was moving past Kato's room, I stumbled against one of the air-conditioning units, making a racket, and almost fell down. I stole past, still clutching my keys, breathing hard, and let myself through the back door. I moved toward the alarm panel and punched in the code to keep it from going off.

I didn't turn on any lights until I got upstairs, into my own room, then I hurried into the bathroom and hopped into the shower.

Not a minute later, I heard the phone ringing. I saw that the bottom light was flashing—the light that corresponded to the Rockingham gate—so I knew it was the limo driver. I figured he'd seen the lights go on in the bedroom and the bathroom and was trying me again. Maybe he thought I'd been asleep. That would be a good thing to tell him: That I'd been asleep.

I let the phone ring, knowing he'd call back, and finished showering. I got out and dried myself, thinking about what I had to do. My bags were pretty well packed, so I was almost ready to go.

I slipped into my black robe and went downstairs and grabbed the Louis Vuitton bag and my golf clubs and took them out front and set them in the courtyard. The driver saw me and got out of the limo, squinting in my direction.

I hurried back upstairs, to finish dressing, with my heart still beating like crazy. I could feel it in my ears, and against my temples, but as I looked around I couldn't understand what I was so worked up about. I took a deep breath and told myself, *The last hour was just a nightmare. None of that ever goddamn happened.*

The phone rang again—the lower light—and I reached for it. "Yeah, man," I said. "I know you're here. I overslept and just got out of the shower. My bags are out front."

I hit the code and opened the front gate, so he could drive through and get the bags, and hung up and finished dressing. Then I hurried downstairs and went outside. The driver was still putting the bags into the trunk of his white limo.

"Hey," I said.

"Good evening, Mr. Simpson."

"We about set here?"

"Yes, sir."

At that moment, Kato showed up, looking spooked. "Did you hear that?" he asked.

"What?" I said.

"That banging noise," he said. "A big thump out back, near the fence."

"I didn't hear shit," I said. "I was in the shower."

"It was a really loud fucking noise, O.J. It scared the hell out of me."

Kato seemed to think that someone had been lurking around that part of the house, and he asked me to have a look, so I humored him. We went off in separate directions, and after about a minute we reconvened near the front door.

"I didn't see anything," I said.

"You got a flashlight?" he asked.

"Jesus, Kato—I'm trying to get out of here. You go look for it and lock up when you're done."

Kato went into the house, still spooked, and I got into the limo and took off. I think the driver was nervous about being late or something, because he got confused at Sunset and took the wrong entry ramp onto the 405 Freeway.

Once we were en route, I called Kato to tell him to make sure to set the alarm. I didn't get through to him, but I remembered having told him to lock up, and I hoped he was smart enough to set the alarm.

"Man," I told the driver. "It feels like I spend my whole life racing to and from airports and getting on and off airplanes."

"I know what you mean," the driver said.

When we got to the airport, I checked in at the curb, like I always do, and watched the skycap tag the bags. A couple of fans came by for autographs, and I was happy to oblige.

On my way to the gate, I signed a few more autographs, and when I boarded the plane I shook hands with a couple more fans. One of them was curious about my ring—he thought it was my Super Bowl ring, but it was actually my Hall of Fame ring—and he took a closer look and admired it. I only mention this because there was supposed to be a cut on my ring finger, but it must have been a phantom cut—there was nothing but a ring there.

I was asleep before the plane took off, and I slept most of the way to Chicago. A limo driver helped me get my bags, then took me to the O'Hare Plaza Hotel. It was quiet at that early hour, even at the airport, and the ride only lasted about five minutes.

I got to my room exhausted, and stripped and immediately fell asleep, but a short time later I was awakened by the ringing phone. I picked it up. It was some cop in Los Angeles—either Philip Vannatter or Thomas Lange, I don't really remember—calling to tell me that he had some bad news. "Nicole has been killed," he said.

"Killed?" I said, not sure I'd heard him correctly. "What do you mean killed?"

And the cop said, "O.J., we can't tell you. But we can tell you that the kids are all right. Where are you?"

I looked around the hotel room and came out of my fog. "I'm in Chicago," I said.

"I need you to come back to L.A. as soon as you can," he said.

Much later, during the trial, the prosecution made a big deal about my response to that phone call, claiming that I never bothered to ask what had happened to Nicole, and suggesting that I didn't ask because I already knew. But that's not the way I remember it. When I was told that Nicole was dead, my first response was the one I just noted: "*Killed? What do you mean killed?*" And even when I was told that I wasn't going to get any more details, I remember asking, "What happened? What the fuck happened?"

The cop repeated himself: "We can't say anything. We're still investigating."

And I said, "And my kids are all right?"

And the cop said, "Yes. As I said, the kids are fine. We need you to come home now, O.J."

"Jesus Christ," I said. "That's all you're going to say: *Come home now!*"

"O.J.," the cop replied. "We'll tell you what we know when you get here. We don't know much ourselves. We'll be waiting for you at your house."

I went nuts, and I remember screaming at him—begging him not to leave me in the dark—but it didn't help. When it became clear that the cops had nothing else to say—either because they didn't want to share anything with me, or because they didn't know much—I slammed the phone down, stormed into the bathroom, and threw a glass across the room. It shattered against the tiled wall, sounding like a gunshot.

I went back into the room and called Cathy Randa, my assistant, and told her what was going on. "I just heard from the cops," I said. "They told me Nicole is dead."

"*Dead?*" she said. "What do you mean dead?"

"I don't know," I replied. "They say she was killed."

"Oh my God!"

I told her to call the cops and get hold of the kids, and asked her to please get me the next flight to Los Angeles.

Then I looked down at my hand and noticed that my finger was bleeding.

I made a few more calls. I called Hertz to tell them I had to go home, I tried calling the cops again, and I called the Browns, down in Dana Point.

Nicole's sister, Denise, got on the phone, hysterical. "You brutal son of a bitch!" she hollered. "You killed her! I know you killed her, you motherfucker!"

Juditha took the phone from her, but I couldn't understand what she was saying. I told her I was getting on the next flight back to Los Angeles, and that I'd speak to her as soon as I landed.

I got dressed and had the porter come up for my bags, then went down to the lobby and asked for a Band-Aid. I guess I'd cut my finger in the bathroom, when I threw that glass.

On my way to the airport, fighting panic, I made a few more calls. I tried to reach Cathy, to see if she knew anything else about my kids, and I again tried to call the cops. For some reason, I even tried to call Kato, back at the house, to see if he knew anything.

When I got to the airport, I was told there was a flight leaving at 7:15, but that it was already booked. I spoke to one of the clerks and she spoke to the manager and they made room for me.

During the course of that entire flight, I sat upright and stock still the entire time. I felt like I was made of glass or something, and that if I moved too much I would shatter into a million pieces. I also remember trying to control my breathing, and thinking that my heart was beating all wrong. I guess I was on the edge of panic.

There was a guy in the seat across the aisle from me, and he noticed and asked me what was wrong. I told him that the cops had just called to tell me that my ex-wife had been killed, and that I didn't even know where my kids were. He turned out to be a lawyer, and after expressing his condolences he gave me some advice: "You should contact your attorney the moment you land," he said. "You're going to need someone to help you navigate your way through this."

Someone? Christ, the man had no idea. I ended up needing a fucking *team* to get me through it, and even then I almost didn't survive.

When the plane landed, I found Cathy Randa waiting for me at the terminal, along with Skip Taft, one of my attorneys. Both Cathy and Skip looked shocked, but probably nowhere near as shocked as I looked.

"Where are my kids?" I said.

"They're safe," Cathy said. "They're on their way to the Browns' place."

"That all your luggage?" Skip asked.

"No, there's the golf clubs—but leave them. I'll get them later."

We hurried through the terminal and talked about what had happened, but they didn't know much more than I did. And I was having trouble hearing them, anyway, because my heart was pounding and the blood was roaring in my ears. I was fucking terrified, to be honest. Nicole was dead—gone forever—and the police were waiting for me at my house.

When we were in the car, leaving the airport, Skip said we should go to his office before we went to see the cops.

"No," I said. "The cops told me they needed to see me, and they said they'd be waiting at my house, and I'm going to my house. I can't go to your office. *I'm going to my house.* That's what the cops asked me to do."

"The cops can wait," he said. "We need to get a handle on this thing."

"No," I said. "I gave them my word. I'm going."

At that point, Skip turned his attention to the radio, and he began flipping through the stations. I picked up bits of information here and there: *Nicole Simpson Brown was dead. There was a second victim, a young man. The murders had taken place in the courtyard of her Bundy condo. Police were waiting to talk to O.J. Simpson, who had been out of town but was apparently on his way home.*

The whole thing felt completely unreal, as if it was happening to someone else, not me. I looked down at my hands. They were shaking uncontrollably. "What the fuck is going on?" I asked Skip. "Are people saying they think *I* did it? I can't believe people would think that of me—that I could do something like that."

Skip told me to relax, that nobody could possibly think I had anything to do with the murders. Cathy also told me not to worry. "Everything's going to be fine," she said.

"Did the kids see anything?" I asked.

"No," Cathy said. "The police took them out back, through the garage."

I felt the bile rising in my throat. It was all I could do to keep myself from being sick. "Call the Browns. Don't let them tell the kids what happened. I want to be the one to tell them. They're my kids."

"I'll call them," Cathy said.

When we got to the house, the place was crawling with cops

and reporters. It was unreal. We drove up to the gate and I could hear the reporters surging behind Skip's car, shouting my name and snapping pictures.

"This is not a good idea," Skip repeated. "We should have gone to my office."

I ignored him. I got out of the car and moved toward the gate, and the reporters kept hollering at me from across the street.

There was a cop standing guard at the gate, and he seemed a little startled to see me.

"You going to let us through?" I said.

"Not the car," he said. "Not anyone but you."

I turned around and saw my friend Bob Kardashian crossing to greet me. I guess he'd been waiting for me there.

"Jesus, O.J.," he said. He looked like he was near tears. "They're not letting us in."

Skip popped the trunk and Bob and Cathy reached for my carry-on bags and followed me back to the gate. Skip, meanwhile, backed out and went off to park the car.

The cop looked at Cathy and shook his head. "Just you," he said.

"But they're with me," I said.

The officer didn't care. He opened the gate just wide enough to let me pass, and left Bob and Cathy behind with the two small bags. The reporters were going crazy, snapping pictures and trying to figure out what was going on.

I looked through the gate, back at Bob—he looked ashen— and when I turned back the cop was reaching for his handcuffs.

"What the fuck are you doing?" I said. "I live here. This is my house."

"I'm sorry, Mr. Simpson. I'm going to have to handcuff you."

"You ain't gonna handcuff me," I said.

"Mr. Simpson—"

"You gonna handcuff me for *what*? I'm not crazy. I want to talk to someone. Who the fuck's in charge here?"

Bob called out from beyond the gate: "What do you want me to do with the bags?"

Hell if I knew. I wasn't thinking about the bags, and I didn't realize what a strange part they'd play in the proceedings in the months ahead. One of them was my famous Louis Vuitton bag, and it gave reporters a lot of *nothing* to write about: *What the fuck happened to the Louis Vuitton bag? What was in the fucking bag? Where was Bob Kardashian going with O.J.'s bag?*

The irony is that I was trying to bring the bags into the house with me. You'd think that if there had been anything incriminating in those bags I wouldn't have tried to lug them inside, but of course nobody wrote that part of the story. Instead, they made a huge fuss about the *missing* bags, and even suggested that Kardashian had walked off with all sorts of evidence, maybe even the bloody knife. Still, not once in the course of the entire trial did the prosecution make any attempt to retrieve the bags, which remained untouched for months on end.

I began to move toward the house, with the cop right on my ass, mumbling about the goddamn cuffs, and when I turned around I saw the horde of reporters across the street, with all sorts of cameras aimed right at us, rolling and pumping. I took a deep breath and figured I shouldn't make a scene. This was my home. I didn't want to see myself on the news later that day, giving a cop a hard time about handcuffing me. I had to keep cool. The only thing that really mattered was finding out exactly what was going on.

I put my hands behind my back and let the guy handcuff me. He led me toward the front door just as Vannatter and Lange came out the house. They introduced themselves, and told me they were in charge of the investigation.

"Well, I'm here," I said. "I got here as fast as I could."

"Thank you for coming," Vannatter said.

"Don't thank me," I said. "Just take these goddamn cuffs off me. You shouldn't be doing this to me in my own home."

At that moment, Howard Weitzman showed up. He's another attorney, and Skip had called him earlier, seeking his advice, I guess. Maybe he was already there, waiting for me, but that was the first I saw him. He looked directly at Vannatter and Lange. "Mr. Simpson is in no condition to talk right now," he said. "He's still in shock."

And I said, "No. I can talk."

Vannatter asked if I minded going downtown with him and his partner, and I said I didn't mind at all.

And Howard said, echoing Skip, "That's not a good idea."

I don't know whether I was in shock or not, but I was in no mood to listen to lawyers. "I'm going with them," I said. "I'm going to do whatever they ask me to do."

Howard was adamant. He didn't want me to talk to those guys, and he was getting pretty hot and bothered about it. "O.J.," he said. "You're making a mistake."

"I'm not going to sit here and try to cover my ass," I replied, getting a little hot and bothered myself. "I've read enough thrillers and watched enough TV movies and seen enough shit on the news to know that the first guy they go to in these types of situations is the spouse or the ex-spouse or the boyfriend. I'm not going to be one of those people who get described as an 'uncooperative witness.'"

Howard tried to tell me that that wasn't the point—that we needed to take a moment to gather our thoughts and to try to figure out where things stood, and that once we had more information I could be the most cooperative witness in the world. But I didn't want to wait that long. I wanted to know what the cops knew, and I wanted to know right away.

"I don't need a lawyer," I told Howard. "I'm innocent."

And yeah, I know what you're thinking: "*Everybody's* innocent! The prisons are filled with guys who didn't do shit!" But that's my point. Half of you think I did it, and nothing will ever make you change your minds. The other half know I didn't do it, and all the evidence in the world—planted or otherwise—isn't going to sway you, either. But this wasn't about that. This was about me, the prime suspect, the accused party, and I did what all accused men do at the moment of truth: I proclaimed my innocence.

Absolutely 100 percent not guilty, Your Honor.

You might remember that phrase. I used it at the beginning of the trial.

I turned to look at Howard again. "I'm going to talk to them," I said. "I don't care about anything else. I want to know exactly what the fuck is going on."

And that was the truth. My wife was dead. I was exhausted. I needed to know what the cops knew. I wanted to get through this thing as quickly as possible, and I wanted desperately to see my kids.

So I got in the car with Vannatter and Lange and we went down to Parker Center for the interview. No bullshit. No lawyers. No interference.

Just me and them.

If it had only been that easy . . .

7.

THE INTERROGATION

On June 13, 1994, a little after 1:30 p.m., I found myself in an interrogation room at Parker Center, in downtown Los Angeles, talking to Philip Vannatter and Thomas Lange, the two cops who were leading the investigation. The interview lasted thirty-two minutes, and the entire transcript follows:

VANNATTER: . . . my partner, Detective Lange, and we're in an interview room in Parker Center. The date is June thirteenth, 1994, and the time is 13:35 hours. And we're here with O.J. Simpson. Is that Orenthal James Simpson?

OJ: Orenthal James Simpson.

VANNATTER: And what is your birth date, Mr. Simpson?

OJ: July ninth, 1947.

VANNATTER: Okay. Prior to us talking to you, as we agreed with your attorney, I'm going to give you your attorney, I'm going to give you your constitutional rights. And I

would like you to listen carefully. If you don't understand anything, tell me, okay?

OJ: All right.

VANNATTER: Okay. Mr. Simpson, you have the right to
remain silent. If you give up the right to remain silent,
anything you say can and will be used against you in a
court of law. You have the right to speak to an attorney
and to have an attorney present during the questioning.
If you so desire and cannot afford one, an attorney will
be appointed for you without charge before questioning.
Do you understand your rights?

OJ: Yes, I do.

VANNATTER: Are there any questions about that?

OJ: (unintelligible).

VANNATTER: Okay, you've got to speak up louder than
that . . .

OJ: Okay, no.

VANNATTER: Okay, do you wish to give up your right to
remain silent and talk to us?

OJ: Ah, yes.

VANNATTER: Okay, and you give up your right to have an
attorney present while we talk?

OJ: Mmm hmm. Yes.

VANNATTER: Okay. All right, what we're gonna do is, we
want to . . . We're investigating, obviously, the death of
your ex-wife and another man.

LANGE: Someone told us that.

VANNATTER: Yeah, and we're going to need to talk to you
about that. Are you divorced from her now?

OJ: Yes.

VANNATTER: How long have you been divorced?

OJ: Officially? Probably close to two years, but we've been apart for a little over two years.

VANNATTER: Have you?

OJ: Yeah.

VANNATTER: What was your relationship with her? What was the—

OJ: Well, we tried to get back together, and it just didn't work. It wasn't working, and so we were going our separate ways.

VANNATTER: Recently you tried to get back together?

OJ: We tried to get back together for about a year, you know, where we started dating each other and seeing each other. She came back and wanted us to get back together, and—

VANNATTER: Within the last year, you're talking about?

OJ: She came back about a year and four months ago about us trying to get back together, and we gave it a shot. We gave it a shot the better part of a year. And I think we both knew it wasn't working, and probably three weeks ago or so, we said it just wasn't working, and we went our separate ways.

VANNATTER: Okay, the two children are yours?

OJ: Yes.

LANGE: She have custody?

OJ: We have joint custody.

LANGE: Through the courts?

OJ: We went through the courts and everything. Everything is done. We have no problems with the kids, we do everything together, you know, with the kids.

VANNATTER: How was your separation? What—

OJ: The first separation?

VANNATTER: Yeah, was there problems with that?

OJ: For me, it was big problems. I loved her, I didn't want us to separate.

VANNATTER: Uh huh. I understand she had made a couple of crime—crime reports or something?

OJ: Ah, we had a big fight about six years ago on New Year's, you know, she made a report. I didn't make a report. And then we had an altercation about a year ago maybe. It wasn't a physical argument. I kicked her door or something.

VANNATTER: And she made a police report on those two occasions?

OJ: Mmm hmm. And I stayed right there until the police came, talked to them.

LANGE: Were you arrested at one time for something?

OJ: No. I mean, five years ago we had a big fight, six years ago. I don't know. I know I ended up doing community service.

VANNATTER: So you weren't arrested?

OJ: No, I was never really arrested.

LANGE: They never booked you or—

OJ: No.

VANNATTER: Can I ask you, when's the last time you've slept?

OJ: I got a couple of hours sleep last night. I mean, you know, I slept a little on the plane, not much, and when I got to the hotel I was asleep a few hours when the phone call came.

LANGE: Did Nicole have a housemaid that lived there?

OJ: I believe so, yes.

LANGE: Do you know her name at all?

OJ: Evia, Elvia, something like that.

VANNATTER: We didn't see her there. Did she have the day off perhaps?

OJ: I don't know. I don't know what schedule she's on.

LANGE: Phil, what do you think? We can maybe just recount last night—

VANNATTER: Yeah. When was the last time you saw Nicole?

OJ: We were leaving a dance recital. She took off and I was talking to her parents.

VANNATTER: Where was the dance recital?

OJ: Paul Revere High School.

VANNATTER: And was that for one of your children?

OJ: Yeah, for my daughter, Sydney.

VANNATTER: And what time was that yesterday?

OJ: It ended about six thirty, quarter to seven, something like that, you know, in the ballpark, right in that area. And they took off.

VANNATTER: They?

OJ: Her and her family—her mother and father, sisters, my kids, you know.

VANNATTER: And then you went your own separate way?

OJ: Yeah, actually she left, and then they came back and her mother got in a car with her, and the kids all piled into her sister's car, and they—

VANNATTER: Was Nicole driving?

OJ: Yeah.

VANNATTER: What kind of car was she driving?

OJ: Her black car, a Cherokee, a Jeep Cherokee.

VANNATTER: What were you driving?

OJ: My Rolls-Royce, my Bentley.

VANNATTER: Do you own that Ford Bronco that sits outside?

OJ: Hertz owns it, and Hertz lets me use it.

VANNATTER: So that's your vehicle, the one that was parked there on the street?

OJ: Mmm hmm.

VANNATTER: And it's actually owned by Hertz?

OJ: Hertz, yeah.

VANNATTER: Who's the primary driver on that? You?

OJ: I drive it, the housekeeper drives it, you know, it's kind of a—

VANNATTER: All-purpose type vehicle?

OJ: All-purpose, yeah. It's the only one that my insurance will allow me to let anyone else drive.

VANNATTER: OK.

LANGE: When you drive it, where do you park it at home? Where it is now, it was in the street or something?

OJ: I always park it on the street.

LANGE: You never take it in the—

OJ: Oh, rarely. I mean, I'll bring it in and switch the stuff, you know, and stuff like that. I did that yesterday, you know.

LANGE: When did you last drive it?

OJ: Yesterday.

VANNATTER: What time yesterday?

OJ: In the morning, in the afternoon.

VANNATTER: Okay, you left her, you're saying, about six thirty or seven, or she left the recital?

OJ: Yeah.

VANNATTER: And you spoke with her parents?

OJ: Yeah, we were just sitting there talking.

VANNATTER: Okay, what time did you leave the recital?

OJ: Right about that time. We were all leaving. We were all leaving then. Her mother said something about me joining them for dinner, and I said no thanks.

VANNATTER: Where did you go from there, O.J.?

OJ: Ah, home, home for a while, got my car for a while, tried to find my girlfriend for a while, came back to the house.

VANNATTER: Who was home when you got home?

OJ: Kato.

VANNATTER: Kato? Anybody else? Was your daughter there, Arnelle?

OJ: No.

VANNATTER: Isn't that her name, Arnelle?

OJ: Arnelle, yeah.

VANNATTER: So what time do you think you got back home, actually physically got home?

OJ: Seven-something.

VANNATTER: Seven-something? And then you left, and—

OJ: Yeah, I'm trying to think, did I leave? You know, I'm always . . . I had to run and get my daughter some flowers. I was actually doing the recital, so I rushed and got her some flowers, and I came home, and then I called Paula as I was going to her house, and Paula wasn't home.

VANNATTER: Paula is your girlfriend?

OJ: Girlfriend, yeah.

VANNATTER: Paula who?

OJ: Barbieri.

VANNATTER: Could you spell that for me?

OJ: B-A-R-B-I-E-R-I.

VANNATTER: Do you know an address on her?

OJ: No, she lives on Wilshire, but I think she's out of town.

VANNATTER: You got a phone number?

OJ: Yeah . . .

VANNATTER: So you didn't see her last night?

OJ: No, we'd been to a big affair the night before, and then I came back home. I was basically at home. I mean, any time I was—whatever time it took me to get to the recital and back, to get to the flower shop and back, I mean, that's the time I was out of the house.

VANNATTER: Were you scheduled to play golf this morning, some place?

OJ: In Chicago.

VANNATTER: What kind of tournament was it?

OJ: Ah, it was Hertz, with special clients.

VANNATTER: Oh, okay. What time did you leave last night, leave the house?

OJ: To go to the airport?

VANNATTER: Mmm hmm.

OJ: About . . . The limo was supposed to be there at ten forty-five. Normally, they get there a little earlier. I was rushing around—somewhere between there and eleven.

VANNATTER: So approximately ten forty-five to eleven.

OJ: Eleven o'clock, yeah, somewhere in that area.

VANNATTER: And you went by limo?

OJ: Yeah.

VANNATTER: Who's the limo service?

OJ: Ah, you have to ask my office.

LANGE: Did you converse with the driver at all? Did you talk to him?

OJ: No, he was a new driver. Normally, I have a regular driver I drive with and converse. No, just about rushing to the airport, about how I live my life on airplanes, and hotels, that type of thing.

LANGE: What time did the plane leave?

OJ: Ah, eleven forty-five the flight took off.

VANNATTER: What airline was it?

OJ: American.

VANNATTER: American? And it was eleven forty-five to Chicago?

OJ: Chicago.

LANGE: So yesterday you did drive the white Bronco?

OJ: Mmm hmm.

LANGE: And where did you park it when you brought it home?

OJ: Ah, the first time probably by the mailbox. I'm trying to think, or did I bring it in the driveway? Normally, I will park it by the mailbox, sometimes . . .

LANGE: On Ashford, or Ashland?

OJ: On Ashford, yeah.

LANGE: Where did you park yesterday for the last time, do you remember?

OJ: Right where it is.

LANGE: Where it is now?

OJ: Yeah.

LANGE: Where, on—?

OJ: Right on the street there.

LANGE: On Ashford?

OJ: No, on Rockingham.

LANGE: You parked it there?

OJ: Yes.

LANGE: About what time was that?

OJ: Eight-something, seven . . . eight, nine o'clock, I don't know, right in that area.

LANGE: Did you take it to the recital?

OJ: No.

LANGE: What time was the recital?

OJ: Over at about six thirty. Like I said, I came home, I got my car, I was going to see my girlfriend. I was calling her and she wasn't around.

LANGE: So you drove the—you came home in the Rolls, and then you got in the Bronco . . .

OJ: In the Bronco, 'cause my phone was in the Bronco. And because it's a Bronco. It's a Bronco, it's what I drive, you know. I'd rather drive it than any other car. And, you know, as I was going over there, I called her a couple of times and she wasn't there, and I left a message, and then I checked my messages, and there were no new messages. She wasn't there, and she may have to leave town. Then I came back and ended up sitting with Kato.

LANGE: Okay, what time was this again that you parked the Bronco?

OJ: Eight-something, maybe. He hadn't done a Jacuzzi, we had . . . Went and got a burger, and I'd come home and kind of leisurely got ready to go. I mean, we'd done a few things . . .

LANGE: You weren't in a hurry when you came back with the Bronco.

OJ: No.

LANGE: The reason I asked you, the cars were parked kind of at a funny angle, stuck out in the street.

OJ: Well, it's parked because . . . I don't know if it's a funny angle or what. It's parked because when I was hustling at the end of the day to get all my stuff, and I was getting my phone and everything off it, when I just pulled it out of the gate there, it's like it's a tight turn.

LANGE: So you had it inside the compound, then?

OJ: Yeah.

LANGE: Oh, okay.

OJ: I brought it inside the compound to get my stuff out of it, and then I put it out, and I'd run back inside the gate before the gate closes.

VANNATTER: O.J., what's your office phone number?

OJ: (gives number)

VANNATTER: And is that area code 310?

OJ: Yes.

VANNATTER: How did you get the injury on your hand?

OJ: I don't know. The first time, when I was in Chicago and all, but at the house I was just running around.

VANNATTER: How did you do it in Chicago?

OJ: I broke a glass. One of you guys had just called me, and I was in the bathroom, and I just kind of went bonkers for a little bit.

LANGE: Is that how you cut it?

OJ: Mmm, it was cut before, but I think I just opened it again, I'm not sure.

LANGE: Do you recall bleeding at all in your truck, in the Bronco?

OJ: I recall bleeding at my house and then I went to the Bronco. The last thing I did before I left, when I was rushing, was went and got my phone out of the Bronco.

LANGE: Mmm hmm. Where's the phone now?

OJ: In my bag.

LANGE: You have it?

OJ: In that black bag.

LANGE: You brought a bag with you here?

OJ: Yeah, it's—

LANGE: So do you recall bleeding at all?

OJ: Yeah, I mean, I knew I was bleeding, but it was no big deal. I bleed all the time. I play golf and stuff, so there's always something, nicks and stuff here and there.

LANGE: So did you do anything? When did you put the Band-Aid on it?

OJ: Actually, I asked the girl this morning for it.

LANGE: And she got it?

OJ: Yeah, 'cause last night with Kato, when I was leaving, he was saying something to me, and I was rushing to get my phone, and I put a little thing on it, and it stopped.

VANNATTER: Do you have the keys to that Bronco?

OJ: Yeah.

VANNATTER: Okay. We've impounded the Bronco. I don't know if you know that or not.

OJ: No.

VANNATTER: —take a look at it. Other than you, who's the last person to drive it?

OJ: Probably Gigi. When I'm out of town, I don't know who drives the car, maybe my daughter, maybe Kato.

VANNATTER: The keys are available?

OJ: I leave the keys there, you know, when Gigi's there because sometimes she needs it, or Gigi was off and wasn't coming back until today, and I was coming back tonight.

VANNATTER: So you don't mind if Gigi uses it, or—

OJ: This is the only one I can let her use. When she doesn't have her car, 'cause sometimes her husband takes her car, I let her use the car.

LANGE: When was the last time you were at Nicole's house?

OJ: I don't go in, I won't go in her house. I haven't been in her house in a week, maybe five days. I go to her house a lot. I mean, I'm always dropping the kids off, picking the kids up, fooling around with the dog, you know.

VANNATTER: How does that usually work? Do you drop them at the porch, or do you go in with them?

OJ: No, I don't go in the house.

VANNATTER: Is there a kind of gate out front?

OJ: Yeah.

VANNATTER: But you never go inside the house?

OJ: Up until about five days, six days ago, I haven't been in the house. Once I started seeing Paula again, I kind of avoid Nicole.

VANNATTER: Is Nicole seeing anybody else that you—

OJ: I have no idea. I really have absolutely no idea. I don't ask her. I don't know. Her and her girlfriends, they go out, you know, they've got some things going on right now with her girlfriends, so I'm assuming something's happening because one of the girlfriends is having a big problem with her husband because she's always saying she's with Nicole until three or four in the morning. She's not. You know, Nicole tells me she leaves her at one thirty or two or two thirty, and the girl doesn't get home until five, and she only lives a few blocks away.

VANNATTER: Something's going on, huh?

LANGE: Do you know where they went, the family, for dinner last night?

OJ: No. Well, no, I didn't ask.

LANGE: I just thought maybe there's a regular place that they go.

OJ: No. If I was with them, we'd go to Toscana. I mean, not Toscano, Pepponi's.

VANNATTER: You haven't had any problems with her lately, have you, O.J.?

OJ: I always have problems with her, you know? Our relationship has been a problem relationship. Probably lately for me, and I say this only because I said it to Ron yesterday at the—Ron Fishman, whose wife is Cora—at the dance recital, when he came up to me and went, "Oooh, boy, what's going on?" and everybody was beefing with everybody. And I said, "Well, I'm just glad I'm out of the mix." You know, because I was like dealing with him and his problems with his wife and Nicole and evidently some new problems that a guy named Christian was having with his girl, and she was staying at Nicole's house, and something was going on, but I don't think it's pertinent to this.

VANNATTER: Did Nicole have words with you last night?

OJ: Pardon me?

VANNATTER: Did Nicole have words with you last night?

OJ: No, not at all.

VANNATTER: Did you talk to her last night?

OJ: To ask to speak to my daughter, to congratulate my daughter, and everything.

VANNATTER: But you didn't have a conversation with her?

OJ: No, no.

VANNATTER: What were you wearing last night, O.J.?

OJ: What did I wear on the golf course yesterday? Some of these kind of pants, some of these kind of pants—I mean I changed different for whatever it was. I just had on some . . .

VANNATTER: Just these black pants?

OJ: Just these . . . They're called Bugle Boy.

VANNATTER: These aren't the pants?

OJ: No.

VANNATTER: Where are the pants that you wore?

OJ: They're hanging in my closet.

VANNATTER: These are washable, right? You just throw them in the laundry?

OJ: Yeah, I got a hundred pair. They give them to me free, Bugle Boys, so I've got a bunch of them.

VANNATTER: Do you recall coming home and hanging them up, or—?

OJ: I always hang up my clothes. I mean, it's rare that I don't hang up my clothes unless I'm laying them in my bathroom for her to do something with them, but those are the only things I don't hang up. But when you play golf, you don't necessarily dirty pants.

LANGE: What kind of shoes were you wearing?

OJ: Tennis shoes.

LANGE: Tennis shoes? Do you know what kind?

OJ: Probably Reebok, that's all I wear.

LANGE: Are they at home, too?

OJ: Yeah.

LANGE: Was this supposed to be a short trip to Chicago, so you didn't take a whole lot?

OJ: Yeah, I was coming back today.

LANGE: Just overnight?

OJ: Yeah.

VANNATTER: That's a hectic schedule, drive back here to play golf and come back.

OJ: Yeah, but I do it all the time.

VANNATTER: Do you?

OJ: Yeah. That's what I was complaining with the driver about, you know, about my whole life is on and off airplanes.

VANNATTER: O.J., we've got sort of a problem.

OJ: Mmm hmm.

VANNATTER: We've got some blood on and in your car, we've got some blood at your house, and sort of a problem.

OJ: Well, take my blood test.

LANGE: Well, we'd like to do that. We've got, of course, the cut on your finger that you aren't real clear on. Do you recall having that cut on your finger the last time you were at Nicole's house?

OJ: A week ago?

LANGE: Yeah.

OJ: No. It was last night.

LANGE: Okay, so last night you cut it.

VANNATTER: Somewhere after the recital?

OJ: Somewhere when I was rushing to get out of my house.

VANNATTER: Okay, after the recital.

OJ: Yeah.

VANNATTER: What do you think happened? Do you have any idea?

OJ: I have no idea, man. You guys haven't told me anything. I have no idea. When you said to my daughter, who said something to me today, that somebody else might have been involved, I have absolutely no idea what happened. I don't know how, why or what. But you guys haven't told me anything. Every time I ask you guys, you say you're going to tell me in a bit.

VANNATTER: Well, we don't know a lot of answers to these questions yet ourselves, O.J., okay?

OJ: I've got a bunch of guns, guns all over the place. You can take them, they're all there. I mean, you can see them. I keep them in my car for an incident that happened a month ago that my in-laws, my wife and everybody knows about that.

VANNATTER: What was that?

OJ: Going down to . . . And cops down there know about it because I've told two marshals about it. At a mall, I was going down for a christening, and I had just left—and it was like three thirty in the morning, and I'm in a lane, and also the car in front of me is going real slow, and I'm slowing down 'cause I figure he sees a cop, 'cause we were all going pretty fast. And I'm going to change lanes, but there's a car next to me, and I can't change lanes. Then that goes for a while, and I'm going to slow down and go around him but the car butts up to me, and I'm like caught between three cars. They were Oriental guys, and they were not letting me go anywhere. And finally I went on the shoulder, and I sped up, and then I held my phone up so they could see the light part of it, you know, 'cause I have tinted windows, and they kind of scattered, and I chased one of them for a while to make him think I was chasing him before I took off.

LANGE: Were you in the Bronco?

OJ: No.

LANGE: What were you driving?

OJ: My Bentley. It has tinted windows and all, so I figured they thought they had a nice little touch.

LANGE: Did you think they were trying to rip you off?

OJ: Definitely, they were. And then the next thing, you know, Nicole and I went home. At four in the morning I got there to Laguna, and when we woke up, I told her about it, and told her parents about it, told everybody about it, you know? And when I saw two marshals at a mall, I walked up and told them about it.

VANNATTER: What did they do, make a report on it?

OJ: They didn't know nothing. I mean, they'll remember me and remember I told them.

VANNATTER: Did Nicole mention that she'd been getting any threats lately to you? Anything she was concerned about or the kids' safety?

OJ: To her?

VANNATTER: Yes.

OJ: From?

VANNATTER: From anybody.

OJ: No, not at all.

VANNATTER: Was she very security conscious? Did she keep that house locked up?

OJ: Very.

VANNATTER: The intercom didn't work apparently, right?

OJ: I thought it worked.

VANNATTER: Oh, okay. Does the electronic buzzer work?

OJ: The electronic buzzer works to let people in.

VANNATTER: Do you ever park in the rear when you go over there?

OJ: Most of the time.

VANNATTER: You do park in the rear.

OJ: Most times when I'm taking the kids there, I come right into the driveway, blow the horn, and she, or a lot of times the housekeeper, either the housekeeper opens or they'll keep a garage door open up on the top of the thing, you know, but that's when I'm dropping the kids off, and I'm not going in. There's times I go to the front because the kids have to hit the buzzer and stuff.

VANNATTER: Did you say before that up until about three weeks ago you guys were going out again and trying to—

OJ: No, we'd been going out for about a year, and then the last six months we've had—it ain't been working, so we tried various things to see if we can make it work. We started trying to date, and that wasn't working, and so, you know, we just said the hell with it, you know.

VANNATTER: And that was about three weeks ago?

OJ: Yeah, about three weeks ago.

VANNATTER: So you were seeing her up to that point?

OJ: It's, it's—seeing her, yeah, I mean, yeah. It was a done deal. It just wasn't happening. I mean, I was gone. I was in San Juan doing a film, and I don't think we had sex since I've been back from San Juan, and that was like two months ago. So it's been like—for the kids we tried to do things together, you know, we didn't really date each other. Then we decided let's try to date each other. We went out one night, and it just didn't work.

VANNATTER: When you say it didn't work, what do you mean?

OJ: Ah, the night we went out it was fun. Then the next night we went out it was actually when I was down in Laguna, and she didn't want to go out. And I said, "Well, let's go out 'cause I came all the way down here to go out," and we kind of had a beef. And it just didn't work after that, you know? We were only trying to date to see if we could bring some romance back into our relationship. We just said, let's treat each other like boyfriend and girlfriend instead of, you know, like seventeen-year-old married people. I mean, seventeen years together, whatever that is.

VANNATTER: How long were you together?

OJ: Seventeen years.

VANNATTER: Seventeen years. Did you ever hit her, O.J.?

OJ: Ah, one night we had a fight. We had a fight, and she hit me. And they never took my statement, they never wanted to hear my side, and they never wanted to hear the housekeeper's side. Nicole was drunk. She did her thing, she started tearing up my house, you know? I didn't punch her or anything, but I . . .

VANNATTER: . . . slapped her a couple of times.

OJ: No, no, I wrestled her, is what I did. I didn't slap her at all. I mean, Nicole's a strong girl. She's a—one of the most conditioned women. Since that period of time, she's hit me a few times, but I've never touched her after that, and I'm telling you, it's five-six years ago.

VANNATTER: What is her birth date?

OJ: May nineteenth.

VANNATTER: Did you get together with her on her birthday?

OJ: Yeah, her and I and the kids, I believe.

VANNATTER: Did you give her a gift?

OJ: I gave her a gift.

VANNATTER: What did you give her?

OJ: I gave her either a bracelet or the earrings.

VANNATTER: Did she keep them or—

OJ: Oh, no, when we split she gave me both the earrings and the bracelet back. I bought her a very nice bracelet—I don't know if it was Mother's Day or her birthday—and I bought her the earrings for the other thing, and when we split, and it's a credit to her—she felt that it wasn't right that she had it, and I said good because I want them back.

VANNATTER: Was that the very day of her birthday, May nineteenth, or was it a few days later?

OJ: What do you mean?

VANNATTER: You gave it to her on the nineteenth of May, her birthday, right, this bracelet?

OJ: I may have given her the earrings. No, the bracelet, May nineteenth. When was Mother's Day?

VANNATTER: Mother's Day was around that . . .

OJ: No, it was probably her birthday, yes.

VANNATTER: And did she return it the same day?

OJ: Oh, no, she—I'm in a funny place here on this, all right? She returned it—both of them—three weeks ago or so, because when I say I'm in a funny place on this it was because I gave it to my girlfriend and told her it was for her, and that was three weeks ago. I told her I bought it for her. You know? What am I going to do with it?

LANGE: Did Mr. Weitzman, your attorney, talk to you anything about this polygraph we brought up before? What are your thoughts on that?

OJ: Should I talk about my thoughts on that? I'm sure eventually I'll do it, but it's like I've got some weird thoughts now. I've had weird thoughts. You know when you've been with a person for seventeen years, you think everything. I've got to understand what this thing is. If it's true blue, I don't mind doing it.

LANGE: Well, you're not compelled at all to take this thing, number one, and number two—I don't know if Mr. Weitzman explained it to you—this goes to the exclusion of someone as much as the inclusion so we can eliminate people. And just to get things straight.

OJ: But does it work for elimination?

LANGE: Oh, yes. We use it for elimination more than anything.

OJ: Well, I'll talk to him about it.

LANGE: Understand, the reason we're talking to you is because you're the ex-husband.

OJ: I know, I'm the number one target, and now you tell me I've got blood all over the place.

LANGE: Well, there's blood at your house in the driveway, and we've got a search warrant, and we're going to go get the blood. We found some in your house. Is that your blood that's there?

OJ: If it's dripped, it's what I dripped running around trying to leave.

LANGE: Last night?

OJ: Yeah, and I wasn't aware that it was—I was aware that I . . . You know, I was trying to get out of the house. I didn't even pay any attention to it, I saw it when I was in the kitchen, and I grabbed a napkin or something, and that was it. I didn't think about it after that.

VANNATTER: That was last night after you got home from the recital, when you were rushing?

OJ: That was last night when I was . . . I don't know what I was . . . I was in the car getting my junk out of the car. I was in the house throwing hangers and stuff in my suitcase. I was doing my little crazy what I do . . . I mean, I do it everywhere. Anybody who has ever picked me up says that O.J.'s a whirlwind, he's running, he's grabbing things, and that's what I was doing.

VANNATTER: Well, I'm going to step out and I'm going to get a photographer to come down and photograph your hand there. And then here pretty soon we're going to take you downstairs and get some blood from you. Okay? I'll be right back.

LANGE: So it was about five days ago you last saw Nicole? Was it at the house?

OJ: Okay, the last time I saw Nicole, physically saw Nicole—I saw her obviously last night. The time before, I'm trying to think . . . I went to Washington, DC, so I didn't see her, so I'm trying to think . . . I haven't seen her since I went to Washington—what's the date today?

LANGE: Today's Monday, the thirteenth of June.

OJ: Okay, I went to Washington on maybe Wednesday. Thursday I think I was in—Thursday I was in Connecticut, then Long Island on Thursday afternoon and all of Friday. I got home Friday night, Friday afternoon. I played, you know—Paula picked me up at the airport. I played golf Saturday, and when I came home I think my son was there. So I did something with my son. I don't think I saw Nicole at all then. And then I went to a big affair with Paula Saturday night, and I got up and played golf Sunday which pissed Paula off, and I saw Nicole at . . . It was about a week before, I saw her at the—

LANGE: Okay, the last time you saw Nicole, was that at her house?

OJ: I don't remember. I wasn't in her house, so it couldn't have been at her house, so it was, you know, I don't physically remember the last time I saw her. I may have seen her even jogging one day.

LANGE: Let me get this straight. You've never physically been inside the house?

OJ: Not in the last week.

LANGE: Ever. I mean, how long has she lived there? About six months?

OJ: Oh, Christ, I've slept at the house many, many, many times, you know? I've done everything at the house, you know? I'm just saying—you're talking in the last week or so.

LANGE: Well, whatever. Six months she's lived there?

OJ: I don't know. Roughly. I was at her house maybe two weeks ago, ten days ago. One night her and I had a long talk, you know, about how can we make it better for the kids, and I told her we'd do things better. And, okay, I can almost say when that was. That was when I—I don't know, it was about ten days ago. And then we . . . The next day I had her have her dog do a flea bath or something with me. Oh, I'll tell you, I did see her one day. One day I went—I don't know if this was the early part of last week, I went 'cause my son had to go and get something, and he ran in, and she came to the gate, and the dog ran out, and her friend Faye and I went looking for the dog. That may have been a week ago, I don't know.

LANGE: (To Vannatter) Got a photographer coming?
VANNATTER: No, we're going to take him up there.
LANGE: We're ready to terminate this at 14:07.

And that was that. We went off to another part of the building, a photographer took a few pictures of the cut on my finger, and the cops gave me a ride back to Rockingham.

We didn't say a word the whole way.

The press was there when I pulled up, and their numbers had grown. I had to fight my way into my own house, with some of the more aggressive reporters practically trampling each other to get at me.

Two dozen people were waiting for me inside, mostly friends and family, and I greeted them in a complete fog. Bob Kardashian and Howard Weitzman were also there, eager to learn how it had gone at Parker Center. They took me aside and asked me to tell them exactly what I'd told the cops. I couldn't remember much, but I remembered getting a little flustered when they asked me what I thought had happened at the condo, like I knew more than I was letting on. That pissed me off a little, to be honest, but I felt like I pretty much kept it together.

Still, I was sure I got some things wrong. I was especially troubled by all this so-called blood all over the place, and in the Bronco in particular. I thought maybe I had cut myself in the house the previous night, rushing around to get ready for the flight to Chicago, but I wasn't real clear on how it had happened, or exactly when. And I'd recently cut myself in the Bronco, reaching for my cellphone charger, but I couldn't remember *how* recently. And hadn't I had cut myself in Chicago when I threw that glass? Or was that an old cut that just got opened up?

Christ, it was hard to keep track of things. I don't know how they expected me to remember so much detail when half the time I couldn't remember what I'd had for dinner the previous night or where I was supposed to be later that day.

The only thing that mattered was that they believe me: I was 100 percent not guilty. They *had* to believe me.

That's not the way it looked to the cops, though—they had spent hours going through every room in the house, looking for evidence—and it's certainly not the way it looked on the news. We went into the den and flipped through the channels. The major networks were all over the story, and they all seemed to be saying the same thing: *O.J. Did It.*

That really threw me. People were starting to think that I was capable of murder. Worse, the media was starting to dissect my relationship with Nicole—a woman I had loved for fifteen years, before everything went to hell. I could already see the story taking shape: *She was leaving him, and he loved her and wanted her back, and when he realized she wasn't coming back he went over to her place and killed her.*

Things were quickly getting out of control.

The press interviewed anybody they could get their hands on, whether it was a passing neighbor near the Bundy condo or a cleaning woman up on Ashford. I didn't realize so many people were so desperate to appear on TV, but I guess that's Hollywood for you.

I also saw plenty of file footage on Yours Truly, documenting my glory days on the football field, my many years as a football analyst, and my various business successes, but the stories always came full circle and ended on me and Nicole: The young waitress I'd swept off her feet when she was barely eighteen. The storybook romance that turned volatile and ended in divorce. And, *endlessly*, this crazy notion that I wanted her back.

Who the fuck were these people, thinking they knew *anything* about my relationship with Nicole?

There'd been a time, almost two years earlier, when Nicole decided she wanted to separate, and, yes—I had fought hard to make her change her mind. But she wouldn't change her mind, and I moved on. Months later she found she was having second thoughts, and she wrote to share them with me:

> O.J. You'll be my one and only "true love." I'm sorry for the pain I've caused you and I'm sorry we let it die. Please let us be a family again, and let me love you—better than I ever have before.

So I tried again, and I put a whole goddamn year into it, and we failed miserably, and when it finally ended I was glad to be out of it. Everyone who knew Nicole and me knew that story, but the reporters didn't want that story—it didn't support their theory. To hear them tell it, I'd been pining for Nicole for the past two years, begging her to come home, and on the night of June 12 I finally snapped.

It was unreal. As I stood there, watching one misguided reporter after another, each of them hammering the same theme, I felt like I was losing my mind.

The real story, as I've told you, was much simpler and much less dramatic. Nicole and I had been together for seventeen years. The first fifteen had been absolutely terrific; the last two had been total hell. Sounds like a lot of marriages, right? But now everything I was hearing about myself was based on a cartoon version of those last two years. I heard myself described as an obsessively jealous ex-husband so many times that the media almost had *me* believing it. To make matters worse, a number of reporters ran around interviewing these so-called experts on battered women, creating the impression that Nicole had been a battered woman, and that I, O.J. Simpson, her former husband, was a known batterer. I remember hearing the phrase "escalating violence" a number of times, and wondering how it applied to us. I realized that anyone listening to those particular reports would come away thinking that there had been some kind of pattern in our marriage—that I had repeatedly beat my wife, and that the beatings had become progressively worse. Jesus! I hadn't even begun to mourn Nicole, and here they were, telling me—and the world—that I'd beat her mercilessly.

Whenever I changed the channel, I'd come across a variation on the same theme. Someone would be talking to another one of these so-called experts about the right way for a woman to leave an abusive man, for example, and I would stand there in shock, open-mouthed, listening. I simply didn't get it. This was a story about my ex-wife, who had just been murdered, and they were turning it into a story about spousal abuse. One expert went through various *scenarios* on the proper way to *escape*—call the police, leave the house while he's at work, get a restraining order—yada yada yada. I had to turn off the TV. It was making me nuts.

The saddest part is, people bought it. *If it was on the news, it had to be true.*

Many months later, when I was sitting in prison, being tried on two counts of murder, I was visited on several occasions by Dr. Lenore Walker, a *real* expert on battered women, and she agreed with what Dr. Bernard Yudowitz had told me—that I did not have the personality of a batterer. She had subjected me to a number of standardized tests, and while I was happy with her conclusion, I've got to tell you—just to be honest here—that those tests were pretty much bullshit. I remember pointing this out to her: "You have some questions on there that don't make any sense at all," I said.

She asked for examples, and I immediately came up with two. The first was, "When you walk into a room, do you think everyone is looking at you?" Fuckin'-A they're looking at me! I don't think it. I *know* it. *Everybody* is looking at me.

The second was, "Do you think you're the subject of conversation in most social situations?" Hell, yeah! I *am* the subject of conversation!

Now, if a guy who sells insurance says that—and I don't have anything against guys who sell insurance—it might mean he's got some kind of personality disorder. Hell, for all I know, it makes him a wife-abuser. But it doesn't mean shit when I say it, because it's the truth. I remember telling Dr. Walker, "It isn't that simple. People are different. I don't see how you can put so much faith in these tests." And I told her this *after* she came to me with the results, *after* she decided I didn't have the makings of an abusive husband.

And I told her this for one very simple reason: I didn't need anyone to tell me that I wasn't abusive, let alone some bogus tests. I *knew* I wasn't abusive.

But that's not what the media wanted to hear. It didn't bolster their story.

As far as they were concerned, I was the one and only suspect, and they were going to make a case against me before I even went to trial.

8.
—

THE FIGHT OF MY LIFE

A T SOME POINT, late that same evening, somebody turned off the TV and urged me to go to bed. The stories were too upsetting and were making me crazy. One minute I'd be crying, the next I'd be on my feet, screaming at the TV set.

I went to bed, but I don't remember sleeping much, and in the morning, with the press still camped outside, Bob decided I should leave the house and move into his place, in Encino. I had to try to get out of the house without being spotted by the media, and I told him about the secret path that cut through Eric Watts' property, over by the tennis courts. Before we left, I asked Kardashian to get me something from under the Bentley's front seat. He went and got it. It was my black grip, with my .357 Magnum inside (though of course he didn't know this). I then packed a few things into my black duffel—some clean clothes, toiletries, et cetera—and we left the house at the same time.

Kardashian drove though the Rockingham gate, and turned toward Ashford, and a few minutes later I met him on Bristol.

None of the reporters had been smart enough to follow him. They all thought I was still inside the house.

I asked him to take me to the airport to pick up my golf bag, which we'd left behind, and I found it right away. The bag was made by Victorinox, the Swiss Army Knife people, and had that distinctive logo. It had been given to me some months earlier by the company, with whom I was doing business.

After we left the airport, we drove straight to Kardashian's house, in Encino, and Bob started talking about the other Bob—Bob Shapiro. He felt that Howard Weitzman wasn't the right guy for us—he wasn't a criminal attorney—and he thought we should see what Shapiro had to say about the situation.

"What are we going to do about Howard?" I asked.

"Let's worry about that later," he said.

When we got to Kardashian's place, my close friend A.C. Cowlings was waiting for us with my kids. They were in one of the guest bathrooms, playing in the Jacuzzi, and when I first saw them I almost fell apart. I hugged both of them and told them we had a lot to talk about, and I asked them to get dressed and come downstairs when they were done.

When they showed up, looking so clean and fresh, I could feel the blood rushing to the back of my throat, and I found myself fighting tears. Again, the whole thing felt unreal. I'd seen the kids less than two days earlier, and they were the same kids, but in that short period of time the whole world had changed. Suddenly I felt very alone. Up until that point, ever since I'd heard the news, I'd either been traveling or in rooms full of people, but now it was just me and the two kids, and I didn't know where to begin.

"Something has happened to Mommy," I began, but Sydney cut me off before I could continue.

"We know," she said. "She's in heaven."

I had assumed that I was going to be the one to break the news, but apparently Judy had already told them.

"That's right," I said. "She's in heaven."

"Can we play a game?" Sydney asked.

I realized that neither of them really understood what had happened to Nicole, let alone the long-term effects that her death would have on their lives. But then, what did I expect? I hadn't processed it either.

They wanted me to read them a story, and I read them a story, and they wanted to play, so we horsed around a little and I tickled them and made them laugh. But it was unbearably hard for me. I was sitting there staring at these kids, knowing that they were never again going to see their mother, and knowing how deeply that was going to affect them for the rest of their lives. That really destroyed me. I was so overwhelmed that I excused myself for a moment and locked myself in the downstairs bathroom and wept. Then I pulled myself together and rejoined them, and the three of us sat there, enjoying each other's company, pretending that everything was just fine—that life was great.

Later that same day, A.C. took the kids back to Dana Point, back to the Browns, and I watched them pull away in his white Bronco and felt all emptied out. As I look back on it now, I believe that that's when it finally hit me—that that was the moment I finally realized Nicole was truly gone.

A short while later Bob Shapiro showed up to talk to me about what lay ahead. He immediately cut to the chase. Almost the first thing he said was, "O.J., I need to know: Did you do this?"

"Absolutely not," I said. "I didn't do it, and I still can't believe it actually happened."

We talked for a couple of hours—Kardashian, Shapiro, and myself—and Shapiro seemed especially upset about the fact that Weitzman had let me talk to the cops. I told him that I had insisted on talking to the cops, and he said that that wasn't the point. Weitzman should have tried to stop me, and—when that didn't work—he should have been at my side for the interrogation.

Shapiro asked me a few more questions—about Sydney's recital, the flight to Chicago, the cut on my hand, et cetera—then got to his feet.

"We have a lot of work ahead of us," he said. "I better get started."

I thanked him and he left, and Kardashian called Weitzman to break the news to him. Weitzman didn't take it well. He began cursing Kardashian, who got tired of trying to explain the situation to him and simply hung up. Not surprisingly, the press found out that Weitzman was no longer representing me, and they even tried to use that against me, suggesting that Weitzman had pulled out because he had doubts about my innocence. I don't know whether he had doubts about my innocence, but I do know that Weitzman didn't pull out—he was *pushed*.

After his conversation with Weitzman, Kardashian called a psychiatrist he knew and asked if he might prescribe a little something to get through the wake and funeral. I spoke to the doctor on the phone. "It's going to get very tough in the days ahead," he said. "I'm going to prescribe something that should keep you from hitting bottom."

The pharmacy delivered the stuff a short while later—sleeping pills, anti-anxiety pills, antidepressants—and I followed the directions. It said the anxiety pills would kick in pretty fast, but that the antidepressants wouldn't take effect for at least a week or two.

When it was time for bed, Kardashian walked me to the room he'd set aside for me and wished me a good night. "I'm glad Shapiro's on board," he said.

"Me too," I said.

I thought about that as I stripped and got into bed. I didn't even know Bob Shapiro, and from the looks of it my life was in his hands—I was in control of absolutely nothing.

I hardly slept again that night, even with the pills. I kept thinking of the kids, and of Nicole, and as I drifted off I vaguely remembered having been told about the wake, which was scheduled for the following afternoon. I was so out of it that I actually remember thinking, *A wake? For whom? Who died?*

In the morning, I turned on the TV and it was the same old shit. The reporters were still harping on this idea that Nicole was leaving me and getting on with her life, and that I'd been unable to handle it. There were also those misguided rumors about Howard Weitzman, and the *real* reasons he had removed himself from the case. I remember thinking that the press got *everything* wrong. I also remember thinking that they got everything wrong really, really fast.

In the middle of yet another report, Kardashian walked into the den and told me that Lou Brown was on the line, calling from Dana Point. I got on the phone and Lou told me that the first viewing was going to be in Laguna Beach, at four that afternoon. I told him that I didn't want an open viewing for anyone other than the direct family. I said I didn't want to see a picture of Nicole in her casket in some tabloid. I said I didn't want the kids to have to live with an image like that for the rest of their lives.

"I want them to remember her just as she was," I said.

"Okay," Lou said.

In the afternoon, a limo arrived to pick me up. Kardashian

went with me. The drive took over an hour, and I don't remember talking much. I think I fell asleep, to be honest. The drugs the shrink had given me were pretty powerful.

I remember waking up as we were pulling into the mortuary parking lot. There were dozens of people there, and dozens of reporters, and I climbed out of the limo and went straight inside without even looking at anyone. All of my kids were there: Jason, Arnelle, Justin, and Sydney. Al Cowlings was with them. I saw Judy and Lou, and we exchanged a few words, and then I went over and took a look at Nicole. She looked as white as a sheet. I leaned over and kissed her, and I could hear Arnelle crying just behind me, and a moment later everyone kind of shuffled out of the room and left me there with Nicole. I don't know how long I was in there. I remember just standing there, shaking my head, still refusing to accept her death, and then I heard someone behind me and turned around. It was Judy. She looked at me and started crying, then asked me, point blank, "O.J., did you do this?"

I didn't even get upset, to be honest. "No," I said. "I could never have done this. I loved her too much."

Much later, Judy went on national television and repeated this story, but long after that, during the civil trial, she told the story but failed to mention my denial. At that point the attorneys played a tape of her television appearance. I guess people remember what they want to remember.

After the viewing, we went to the Browns' for a little while—I was in a complete fog, and I only know I was there because I was told I was there—then I got back into the limo for the ride home. I remember that part: I cried all the way.

Kardashian tried to comfort me, but he was pretty broken up himself. He didn't know what to say because there wasn't much he could say.

By the time we got back to Kardashian's place, in Encino, I was in terrible shape. For the first time in my life, I thought about killing myself. I felt sorrowful and angry at the same time, and most of all I felt hopeless. I felt like I had nothing to live for. I felt like my life no longer made any sense.

At some point I fell asleep—I was exhausted and all hollowed out and I took a couple of extra sleeping pills—and when I woke up the following morning, groggy and disoriented, I felt more depressed than ever. I went downstairs and found Kardashian in the kitchen, and I tried to revive myself with coffee. A.C. showed up while I was in the middle of my second cup. He had brought a suit for me to wear to the funeral.

I went upstairs and it took me a very long time to get dressed. I couldn't seem to make my arms work. They felt heavy and sore, like they would if you overdid it in the gym.

The funeral took place at St. Martin of Tours, a church on the corner of Sunset and Saltair, in Brentwood. I couldn't have made it through the service without A.C. and Kardashian. Kardashian led me to some seats in the second row, behind the Browns, and I remember that they turned to look at me. They weren't smiling.

My four kids joined me, and at that point I think Sydney was beginning to understand what had happened. Justin, on the other hand, was completely oblivious.

I noticed pictures of Nicole and the children resting on the casket, then looked beyond the casket and saw a literal wall of cameras pointed in my general direction. I had no idea that the press was going to be allowed inside, but I didn't have the energy to complain. And who was I going to complain to anyway?

I couldn't follow the service, to be honest. At one point I thought it was over, and I found myself standing, shaking a lot of hands, thanking people, but then I was sitting again, and I looked up and saw that Judy Brown was preparing to deliver a eulogy. I don't remember that, either, but I know it was short.

After the service, people came up to talk to me, and to shake my hand and hug me, and I went through the motions and nodded from time to time, trying not to fall apart. Once again, I felt like none of this was really happening, that I was in the middle of a horrible, unimaginable dream, but when I stepped into the parking lot I knew it was no dream. There was an army of reporters across the street, and half-a-dozen helicopters overhead, and I could hear some of them shouting my name.

"O.J., right here!" "O.J., can we ask you a few questions?" "O.J., can we get a shot of you with the kids?"

It took about an hour to get to the cemetery, in Mission Viejo, and the press followed us down. So did the helicopters. Strangely enough, that's what I remember most clearly about the funeral—the damn helicopters, making a racket overhead, not giving a shit about any of us. I also remember, vaguely, sitting through a short service, and I vaguely remember the priest, but I can't remember a single specific detail about anything at all. I guess those drugs were working pretty hard.

Later, some reporter said that I stood by the grave for a long time after the service, alone, talking to Nicole, and he suggested that I was asking for forgiveness. I don't know where he got that idea. I didn't stand by the grave for more than a half a minute. I had my kids with me, and they never left my side. That much I do remember.

The next thing I remember was being back in the limo, on our way to the Browns, and it felt almost like a time-cut in a movie—I wasn't sure how I had gotten there. On the other hand, during the drive Justin spotted a Wendy's hamburger place, and announced that he was hungry. Sydney said she was hungry, too, so we pulled up to the drive-thru window and I ordered food for everyone.

I remember looking at my kids, at their smiling faces, and at the way they attacked their burgers, and thinking, *It's the little things in life that keep you going.*

An hour later, I wasn't sure if I could keep going. Or whether I wanted to.

I got back to Encino late that night and turned on the news. There was footage of us at the church, and more footage of us at the cemetery, but I couldn't watch it without crying.

I popped a couple of pills and went to bed.

The following morning, Friday, I got out and took a leak and went right back to bed. There was a remote next to the bed and I picked it up and turned on the TV. There was some kind of action movie on, and I watched for a few seconds, but then I heard a knock at the door and killed the picture.

"Come in," I said.

Kardashian walked inside with Robert Shapiro. We made a little small talk—they asked me how I'd slept and stuff—and then they cut to the chase.

"I heard from the police this morning," Shapiro said.

"Yeah?"

"They've issued a warrant for your arrest. You're supposed to turn yourself in at eleven."

I looked at the clock on the night table next to the bed. It was almost ten. I had an hour.

"Okay," I said. "I'll shower and get dressed."

Shapiro then told me that a couple of doctors were on their way to the house, to collect blood and hair samples for the police. I felt like I was in the middle of an episode of a bad TV movie, only it wasn't a movie. I just shrugged. I was too numb to say anything.

Kardashian broke the awkward silence. "A.C. and Paula are downstairs," he said.

"Okay," I said. "I'll get ready."

Then Shapiro spoke again. "O.J.," he said, "it's just you and us in this room at the moment, and I don't know if we'll get another chance like this. I need to know. Is there anything you want to tell us?"

"No," I said. "I've told you everything. I'm not hiding anything. You know everything I know, and everything I've told you is the truth."

Shapiro didn't look real happy about my response, but he didn't push. He told me that the doctors would be there any minute, and that he'd wait for me downstairs, and then he left the room.

I looked over at Kardashian. He smiled this sort of sad smile, and for some crazy reason he started talking about our long friendship, and about all the great times we'd shared over the years. I didn't understand what he was trying to tell me. Was he saying the good times were over?

"Yeah," I said. "We sure had some good old times."

He looked like he was about to cry. "I'll wait for you downstairs," he said, then turned and quickly left the room.

Much later, I heard a crazy story about this incident. Supposedly, I noticed a tape recorder on the night table next to the bed, and the moment Kardashian left the room I picked it up and started talking about my life. I talked about my kids, and about how much I loved them; I talked about Nicole and about how much she had meant to me and about how much I missed her already; and I talked about the fact that I believed myself to be a good person, a man who had always tried to do right by others. It was a good story, but I don't know where it came from. I'm not saying it couldn't have happened, but I don't remember a tape recorder, and I don't remember review-ing my life. Still, who knows? At that point I was so drugged up I could hardly find my way into the shower. But if it did hap-pen, and if someone has the tape, I'd love to hear it someday.

I eventually found my way into the shower, and I eventually got dressed.

When I got downstairs, the place was crawling with people. Paula looked up and started crying the moment she saw me. A.C. was there, too, and so was the psychiatrist. He asked me how I felt and told him I was fine, but I should have told him the truth: I felt hopelessly lost.

Then the doctors showed up to collect their samples. One of them was Henry Lee and the other was Michael Baden. They had a nurse with them, and I think I sat down and she took some blood. She took a lot of blood. I think she must have filled up four or five glass vials.

When she was done, I said I needed a moment to myself, and I excused myself and disappeared into the den. I called Judy Brown and told her that she needed to take care of the kids till this was resolved, then I called Skip Taft, one of my lawyers, and asked him to work out the details with the Browns.

When we got off the phone, I found a legal pad and wrote a letter, in longhand, that filled four entire pages. I folded the let-ter and put it in an envelope and sealed the envelope and wrote across the front: "To Whom It May Concern."

I left the room and gave it to Kardashian and told him not to open it till after.

"After what?" he said.

"Just after," I said. I didn't honestly know what I meant myself. "When the time comes, you'll know." I'm not sure what I meant by that, either, but it sounded right.

The doctors were still there—I think they still wanted a hair sample or something, and they were interested in taking another look at the cut on my hand—so I gave them what they needed.

Then Shapiro said it was time to go. "I gave the cops my word that I'd have you at Parker Center at eleven, and it's already after eleven," he said.

"I don't give a shit," I said. "What can they do to me now?"

I think Shapiro went off to call the cops to tell them that we were running a little late, but that we'd be there shortly.

I went over and asked Paula to please leave before me. I don't know why, but I guess I thought that would make it easier on both of us. She'd be leaving because I had asked her to leave, instead of standing there, watching me walk away from her life. I'm not sure that made any sense, either then or now, but at that point nothing made much sense.

Paula didn't want to leave, but I asked her again, and she finally relented and I asked A.C. to walk her out to her car.

I went back to the guestroom and got my black grip. My Magnum was inside, along with my passport, about ten dollars in cash, and some pictures of Nicole and the kids. I looked at the pictures and started to cry, but there was a knock at the door and I dried my tears and tried to pull myself together.

"Come in," I said.

Kardashian walked in. "How you holding up?" he asked me.

"Okay," I said.

"Shapiro's waiting downstairs," he said.

"I know," I said.

"Take your time," he said, but he didn't really mean it.

He left the room.

A few minutes later, still carrying my grip, I went downstairs and saw A.C. standing in the foyer, near the front door. I guess everyone else was in the den or something, watching the news.

"Let's get out of here," I said.

"What do you mean?" he said.

"Let's just go," I said.

I walked out the front door and he followed me, and we climbed into his Bronco and pulled out. He didn't say anything. He was my friend. He would do anything for me, and I would have done anything for him.

"Let's go by the house," I said.

"What house?" he said.

"Nicole's house," I said.

He didn't ask why. He got onto the 405 Freeway and headed north. We got off at Sunset, and worked our way toward Bundy, but as we got closer we saw that most of the street was blocked off, and that the place was crawling with cops. I told him to forget it and asked him to take me to the cemetery, and he looked at me, wondering why. "I was so overmedicated that I don't remember a thing," I said. "I want to see the grave before they lock me up. I may never get another chance to see it."

We drove south to Mission Viejo, with me in the back seat, where I could lie down and close my eyes. We didn't talk. Each of us was alone with his thoughts. I found myself thinking back to what Nicole had told me that night in Laguna, right after Mother's Day, when it was clear that we weren't going to be able to save our marriage.

"Maybe we tried to get back together too soon," she had said. She looked incredibly sad. Just remembering the look on her face made me feel like crying.

I also remembered driving back to Los Angeles that night, and helping her put the kids to bed at her place. And I remembered the way she invited me into her bedroom and asked me to make love to her. It was the last time we made love, and just thinking about it was absolutely devastating. I had really loved that girl. Why hadn't we been able to make it work? What had we done wrong? How do other people do it?

As we got close to the cemetery, A.C. called my name and I opened my eyes. There were cops everywhere. He drove around to the far side to see if there was another way in, but there were cops there, too.

"They're looking for you," he said.

I reached across the front seat and turned on the radio, and it turned out he was right. I heard myself described as "a fugitive."

A.C. drove another half-mile or so and pulled into an orange grove, where no one could spot us, not even from the sky. He got out to take a leak, and the moment he left the Bronco I reached for my grip. I unzipped it and pulled out the Magnum. I was in tremendous pain, and I saw nothing but more pain ahead of me, and I decided to end it. I realized, *I can make this stop. One shot to the fucking head and it's over.*

Strangely enough, at that very moment Bob Kardashian was on national television telling the world about my pain. When it appeared that I wasn't going to turn myself in, he had opened the four-page note I'd written earlier that day, and couldn't believe what he was reading. I had asked him to not to open it till *after*, and I guess he thought the time had come. If I hadn't killed myself yet, I was probably about to.

I'm not going to lie to you. I *had* been thinking about killing myself. The first time it crossed my mind was after my brief conversation with Sydney and Justin, at Kardashian's house, when I tried to break the horrible news about Nicole.

"We know," Sydney had said, cutting me off. "She's in heaven."

That just about destroyed me. The pain was unbearable. But I kept going.

But that morning the pain was back, worse that ever. And

since I did not believe I was going to survive it, I had taken the time to sit down and share some final thoughts.

Kardashian was then in the process of sharing those thoughts with the world:

> To whom it may concern: First, everyone understand I have nothing to do with Nicole's murder. I loved her, always have and always will. If we had a problem, it's because I loved her so much.
>
> Recently, we came to the understanding that for now we were not right for each other, at least for now. Despite our love we were different, and that's why we mutually agreed to go our separate ways. It was tough splitting for a second time, but we both knew it was for the best.
>
> Inside I had no doubt that in the future we would be close as friends or more. Unlike what has been written in the press, Nicole and I had a great relationship for most of our lives together. Like all long-term relationships, we had a few downs and ups. I took the heat New Year's 1989 because that's what I was supposed to do. I did not plead no contest for any other reason but to protect our privacy and was advised it would end the press hype.
>
> I don't want to belabor knocking the press, but I can't believe what is being said. Most of it is totally made up. I know you have a job to do, but as a last wish, please, please, please, leave my children in peace. Their lives will be tough enough.
>
> I want to send my love and thanks to all my friends. I'm sorry I can't name every one of you, especially A.C., man, thanks for being in my life. The support and friendship I received from so many: Wayne Hughes, Lewis Markes, Frank Olson, Mark Packer, Bender, Bobby Kardashian.

I wish we had spent more time together in recent years. My golfing buddies, Hoss, Alan Austin, Mike, Craig, Bender, Wyler, Sandy, Jay, Donnie, thanks for the fun. All my teammates over the years, Reggie, you were the soul of my pro career. Ahmad, I never stopped being proud of you. Marcus, you've got a great lady in Catherine, don't mess it up. Bobby Chandler, thanks for always being there. Skip and Kathy, I love you guys, without you I never would have made it through this far. Marguerite, thanks for the early years. We had some fun. Paula, what can I say? You are special. I'm sorry we're not going to have our chance. God brought you to me I now see. As I leave, you'll be in my thoughts.

I think of my life and feel I've done most of the right things. Whatever the outcome, people will look and point. I can't take that. I can't subject my children to that. This way they can move on and go on with their lives. Please, if I've done anything worthwhile in my life, let my kids live in peace from you (press).

I've had a good life. I'm proud of how I lived. My mama taught me to do unto others. I treated people the way I wanted to be treated. I've always tried to be up and helpful so why is this happening? I'm sorry for the Goldman family. I know how much it hurts.

Nicole and I had a good life together. All this press talk about a rocky relationship was no more than what every long-term relationship experiences. All her friends will confirm that I have been totally loving and understanding of what she's been going through. At times I have felt like a battered husband or boyfriend but I loved her, make that clear to everyone. And I would take whatever it took to make it work.

Don't feel sorry for me. I've had a great life, great friends. Please think of the real O.J. and not this lost person.

Thanks for making my life special. I hope I helped yours.

Peace and love, O.J.

I had meant what I'd written. I'd had a wonderful life, but it was over now. It was time to check out.

I looked at the Magnum in my lap and checked to make sure it was loaded. It was.

And just then I heard Dan Rather's voice on the radio: "We have now learned that the police have been to Mr. Simpson's house six or seven times on domestic abuse calls."

And I just goddamn snapped:

"What the fuck, motherfucker!"

And that's when A.C. got back to the truck, still zipping up his fly, and saw the Magnum in my hand. And I guess he snapped, too—though for different reasons. "Man, put that fucking gun down!" he shouted "What the fuck do you think you're doing with that thing?"

But I wasn't listening to him. I was listening to more of Dan Rather's bullshit: "We're now learning that Mr. Simpson has a long history with the Los Angeles Police Department," yada yad yada.

And I'm shouting at the radio, "You ain't learned shit, mother-fucker!"

I almost put a bullet though the radio.

"What the fuck is going on?!" A.C. said, also hollering.

"Nothing!" I said. "Take me the fuck home! That changes everything. I'm not going to listen to any more of this bullshit!"

And A.C. got behind the wheel and pulled out, with me still

fuming and venting. "Who the fuck do these people think they are?! They're supposed to be *reporters*. They hear one lie and if it's a lie they like they goddamn share it with the world. Well, I'm sick to death of it!"

I wasn't thinking of killing myself anymore.

Depression had given way to rage.

And we pulled out of the orange grove, heading back toward the freeway, and he picked up his cellphone and dialed 911. "This is Al Cowlings," he said. "I've got O.J. Simpson with me, and I'm bringing him in."

And wouldn't you know it—must have been some kind of cop GPS—the police were on our tail in minutes. The cemetery wasn't two miles behind us and they were already crawling up our asses.

And A.C. said, "Maybe we should pull over."

And I said, "No fucking way! You told them you were bringing me in, so bring me in already. Take me back to my house."

I was feeling angry. *Defiant*. The rage was fueling me. I was ready to take on the world.

There were more cops now, still following, and I leaned close to the window and looked up into the sky. I think I counted half-a-dozen choppers.

When we were still a few miles from Brentwood, on the 405 Freeway, heading north, it seemed as if the whole world had turned out to watch. People were hanging off overpasses, cheering, holding up signs. *GO JUICE!*

I remember thinking, *When did they have time to make those signs?*

By that point, there were maybe a dozen squad cars with us, behind the Bronco, up ahead of us, on either side. A.C. didn't like it, and he slowed to a crawl. "O.J.," he said. "I'm pulling over."

"No you're not," I said. "You're taking me home."

I put the Magnum to my head, so the cops could see it, and A.C. again used his cellphone to call the cops. "Back the fuck off," he said. "Can't you see the man's gonna kill himself?"

The whole thing took less than an hour. By then we were driving past the Wilshire off-ramp, and A.C. took the Sunset exit. If the cops had any doubts about where we were going, they knew now: O.J. Simpson was heading home.

For a moment, cruising those familiar streets, I suddenly felt crushingly depressed again. A man spends his whole life trying to figure out what it all means, trying to make some sense of this business of living, and in the end he doesn't understand shit.

I missed Nicole. I was worried about the kids.

There was a goddamn battalion waiting for us at Rockingham, and before A.C. had even killed the engine the cops had pretty much surrounded us.

I was pissed off again. What the fuck did they think I was going to do? Shoot it out?

I dialed 911. "You tell those motherfuckers to back off!" I said.

The operator patched me through to someone at the scene, and I hollered at him for a while, but I couldn't see who I was talking to, and I'm not sure what I was trying to say.

Then I saw a sniper on the roof of a neighbor's house, and I swear to God—I almost lost it. The sons of bitches. What were they planning on doing? Taking me out when I stepped out of the Bronco?

I showed them the Magnum again, and I could see the cops tensing up, backing off.

"Put that fucking gun down," A.C. said. "You want to die?"

"I don't know," I said. "Maybe."

And I didn't know, to be honest. I was depressed. Then I was angry. Then I was depressed again. The shrink had told me that the pills were going to keep me from hitting bottom, but this felt awful close to bottom. And if bottom was worse than this, I didn't want to know about it.

A moment later, I felt the tears coming.

"We should have tried harder," I said.

"What's that?"

"Nicole and me," I said. "*I* should have tried harder. Even when I thought I didn't love her, I loved her. It's just there were times I forgot."

A.C. didn't say anything, but I wasn't even looking at him. I was thinking about all those years with Nicole, most of them so good I wasn't sure I deserved them, and I was thinking about the way we'd gone and fucked everything up.

Like I said earlier, this is a love story, and like a lot of love stories it doesn't have a happy ending.

I got out of the Bronco and the cops moved in. They gave me a few minutes in the house, a chance to freshen up, then took me downtown, to Parker Center. They booked me and took my prints and had me pose for a mug shot. The flash blinded me, and I closed my eyes for a few seconds.

Nicole had written:

I want to be with you! I want to love you and cherish you, and make you smile. I want to wake up with you in the mornings and hold you at night. I want to hug and kiss you everyday. I want us to be the way we used to be. There was no couple like us.

And I'm thinking:
You were sure right about that, Nic.
There was no couple like us.

—

AFTERWORD

Dominick Dunne

IT WAS HARD for me to read this mystifying book by O.J. Simpson, although it is so in his character to have become involved in a crooked scheme to make money on his murders and at the same time defraud the Goldman family of the money the civil trial awarded them. Simpson craves the attention he has irretrievably lost. America rejected his acquittal. There were few victory cheers for him. Overnight, he became unwelcome. One of his many high-priced lawyers, Peter Neufeld, said it was "unconscionable" that he was not received back in the Brentwood community where he lived. No, it wasn't unconscionable at all. Who wants to have a two-time killer living in the neighborhood? What was unconscionable was the pack of high-priced lawyers and expert witnesses, the so-called *Dream Team*, who worked so hard and were paid so much to win an acquittal for a man they all knew had murdered two people: his beautiful former wife, Nicole Brown Simpson, the mother of two of his children who were there at the time, allegedly asleep when the slaughter happened, and Ronald Goldman, an acquaintance of Nicole's who unexpectedly appeared at the moment of murder on a good deed to return a pair of glasses that Nicole's mother had left behind at a restaurant where he was a waiter. Ron was a young good-looking guy. He had ambition and big plans for himself in his future, all of which were stabbed out of him by O.J. Simpson.

I was in the courtroom every day of the Simpson trial for almost a year, and I became obsessed with Simpson and the terrible thing he had done. The photographs I was shown during the trial of Nicole's nearly-severed head and Ron Goldman's mutilated body will haunt me until the last day of my life. Simpson's savagery that terrible night of June 12th, 1994 knew no limits. Of course the Goldmans hated him. I hated him too. Now, thirteen years later, I still feel my deep sense of hatred toward him whenever I see him on television. Once he was a handsome champion. Now his face has become the face of a failure.

Judge Lance Ito has taken a lot of heat over the years for allowing Johnnie Cochran, the head of Simpson's so-called Dream Team, to usurp his powers and take over the courtroom as his own, but Judge Ito had many good points that should not go unheralded. One that I admired was his sensitivity for the feelings of the victims' families. Media demands for seats in the courtroom came from all over the world and exceeded by far the number of seats available. I arrived in Los Angeles from New York a few days before the start of the trial. The following, slightly edited, is taken directly from my diary on the day when I met Judge Ito. I later used a version of my diary in my book about the Simpson trial called *Another City Not My Own.*

On the day Jerrianne Hayslett, who was in charge of media relations for Judge Ito, posted the seating arrangements for the media, there were screams of disappointment from those who had to share seats, or did not get seated at all in the courtroom. To my astonishment, I received a permanent seat in the front row that I did not have to share for alternate periods with other reporters. I could feel there was a great deal of resentment toward me, the out-of-towner. The Los Angeles Times sneeringly referred to me as "celebrity author," and I was referred to more mockingly by a Copley News reporter as "Judith Krantz in pants." The famous defense attorney Leslie Abramson referred to my books as "jumped-up romance novels." I didn't care. I had my seat. That was all that mattered to me.

"Judge Ito would like to see you in chambers," said Deputy Jex a few days later in the snarling tone of voice he used when speaking to members of the media. I wouldn't have minded his unpleasantness so much if he had been equally unpleasant to the defendant on trial for a double murder. Instead, he spoke to Simpson in the fawning manner of a fan at a Buffalo Bills game. It was the first time that I had met Judge Ito, who was shortly to spring to national prominence and the cover of Newsweek magazine.

"Sit down, Mr. Dunne," he said, motioning me to a sofa opposite his desk. "I've read some of your coverage of the Menendez trial. You certainly take a very definite stand. There's no mistaking how you feel about those two brothers."

I am, after all, a victims' advocate. I felt the same passion against Simpson as I had against the Menendez brothers, who fired sixteen shots from two 12-gauge shotguns into their father's and mother's bodies.

"It's come to my attention that there are some people who are giving you a hard time because of your seat in the courtroom," he said.

"I can handle that, Your Honor," I replied.

"You must understand that they're giving me a hard time as well because of your seat in the courtroom," he said.

For a minute, I thought the judge was going to take my seat away from me.

He continued, "I would like you to know that I assigned you that seat. That seat is yours for the length of the trial."

"Thank you, Your Honor. I am very grateful."

Ito stood up, indicating that the meeting was over. "Have you ever seen anything like this, Mr. Dunne?" He was referring to the massive media event that the trial was becoming.

"No, I haven't, Your Honor, and I've covered a lot of high-profile trials."

The judge looked me squarely in the eye. "You see, I felt very safe giving you a seat next to the Goldman family and the Brown family. I knew that you would know how to deal with the families, that you wouldn't intrude on them or ask questions."

I understood the judge's look and words. I knew that he realized that I, like Louis Brown, the father of Nicole, and Fred Goldman, the father of Ron, was the father of a murdered child.

"Thank you, Your Honor," I said as I went out the door.

In 1982, my daughter, Dominique, aged 22, was strangled to death by a former boyfriend who stalked her and killed her. Costumed as a sacristan in a Catholic monastery, he read the Bible throughout the trial, a cheap courtroom trick that fooled the jury. I experienced inner rage when the killer received a sentence of a mere six years, which was cut to three years on the day of the sentencing. Before dismissing the jury, the judge thanked them on behalf of both families. I stood up in the courtroom and screamed at the judge, "Don't thank them on behalf of my family, Judge Katz." I was removed from the court by two bailiffs. The killer was released after two and a half years. I was so crazed with grief and anger that I went to a private detective on lower Sunset Boulevard to inquire about hiring a killer to kill my daughter's killer. Of course, I would never have gone through with it, even if the private detective hadn't talked me out of it. I wrote about it instead and brought a halt to the career of the judge.

The point of telling you this is that I totally understand the rage of Fred Goldman and the hatred he felt for O.J. Simpson and Johnnie Cochran. I had had my own version of what Fred Goldman and his wife and daughter were going through. We became so close during those ten months that I was not afraid to tell Fred when he went too far in his media outbursts. He was fearless. The outraged public cheered him. He was the only one who dared take on the formidable Johnnie Cochran, whom I believe would have instigated riots in the city if Simpson had been found guilty. Among the many things I admired about Fred Goldman was how articulate he was when he stood before the news cameras. He was a man to be reckoned with. I also became enormously close to Fred's wife, Patti, and his daughter, Kim. I understood the Goldmans, and the Goldmans understood me, and we became friends.

A lot of the time, I sat next to Kim. What a wonderful young heartbroken woman she was. What a sister she must have been to Ron. I adored her like the daughter I had lost to murder. We whispered to each other throughout the day about what was going on in front of us. One day, she told me she couldn't stand it when I referred to O.J. Simpson as O.J. when I talked about him. She said it was too familiar, too friendly. I thought so too. It didn't work for us to call him Simpson. I said to Kim, "What about referring to him as the killer when we talk?" From then on, whenever he entered the courtroom, we'd say to each other, "Here comes the killer."

We all should have known when the long-sequestered jury only deliberated for a couple of hours after a ten month trial that something was amiss, especially when several of the jurors had arrived at the deliberation with their bags packed. The utter shock of hearing the words "Not Guilty" became a never-to-be-forgotten moment in all of our lives. The Court TV camera cut to the Goldmans, Kim's tear-stained face was buried in her devastated father's chest. On camera, my mouth was hanging open in disbelief. I love the Goldman family and whatever they do to destroy Simpson, even turning his own book, *If I Did It*, against him has my full backing.

DOMINICK DUNNE
August 2007

RESOURCES

E VERY MINUTE OF every day, a violent crime occurs in this country. Over the past year, approximately 17,520 people were murdered. That's two people every hour.

Last year, there were more than 300,000 rapes *reported*. That's 34 rapes per hour. This past year, there were also more than 300,000 *reported* sexual assaults on children. Again, that's more than 34 per hour. We can't even begin to imagine how many are not reported.

Every year, there are millions of crimes committed against innocent, law-abiding citizens. Approximately 2% of our population commits 100% of the violent crimes, leaving the remaining 98% of us the potential victims. And our system seems to focus on and care more about the accused and the convicted than the rest of us. We need to band together and protect each other from these predators who seek to wreak havoc on our society.

We must arm ourselves with the knowledge and power that we can make a difference, confident that our voices matter and committed to not sit back and do nothing. Regardless of whether you have been directly impacted by crime or not, eventually we will all be touched by crime on some level. You cannot pretend it doesn't exist just because it hasn't happened to you. We wouldn't wish this horrific pain on anyone, but we have to be prepared as best we can, and we need to be there for one another.

The following organizations have committed themselves to being a support system for people who have been traumatized and victimized. Each is dedicated to empowering victims to become survivors and to move through their tragedies with as much grace, dignity, and strength as possible.

These are resources the Goldman Family highly recommends. Their inclusion on this list does not necessarily represent support for this book.

The National Organization for Victim Assistance (NOVA)

NOVA is a private non-profit 501(c)(3) organization of victim and witness assistance programs and practitioners, criminal justice agencies and professionals, mental health professionals, researchers, former victims and survivors, and others committed to the recognition and implementation of victim rights and services.

Founded in 1975, NOVA is the oldest national group of its kind in the worldwide victims' movement. NOVA's mission is to promote rights and services for victims of crime and crisis everywhere.

Information and Referrals for Victims of Crime and Disaster
24 hours a day, 7 days a week.

Phone: 1-800-TRY-NOVA (6682)
(703) 535-NOVA (6682)
www.trynova.org

Parents of Murdered Children (POMC)

POMC makes a difference through ongoing emotional support, education, prevention, advocacy, and awareness. Their vision is to provide support and assistance to all survivors of homicide victims while working to create a world free of murder.

National POMC
100 East Eighth Street, Suite 202
Cincinnati, Ohio 45202
Toll Free: (888) 818-POMC (7662)
Phone: (513) 721-5683
Fax: (513) 345-4489
natlpomc@aol.com
www.pomc.org

The Office for Victims of Crime (OVC)

OVC is committed to enhancing the nation's capacity to assist crime victims and to providing leadership in changing attitudes, policies, and practices to promote justice and healing for all victims of crime.

Office for Victims of Crime Resource Center
National Criminal Justice Reference Service
P.O. Box 6000
Rockville, MD 20849
Phone: 1-800-851-3420
TTY: 1-877-712-9279
www.ojp.usdoj.gov/ovc/

National Center for Victims of Crime

The mission of the National Center for Victims of Crime is to forge a national commitment to help victims of crime rebuild their lives. It is dedicated to serving individuals, families, and communities harmed by crime.

National Center for Victims of Crime
2000 M Street NW, Suite 480
Washington, DC 20036
Phone: (202) 467-8700
Fax: (202) 467-8701
www.ncvc.org

The National Domestic Violence Hotline

Phone: 1-800-799-SAFE (7233)
TTY: 1-800-787-3224
www.ndvh.org

Crime Survivors

Crime Survivors' vision is for victims of crime to recover from their experience mentally, physically, emotionally, and financially by receiving respect, support, and protection from law enforcement, the judicial system, and the community.

Crime Survivors, Inc.
PO Box 54552
Irvine, CA 92619
Phone: (949) 872-7895
Fax: (775) 245-4798
www.crimesurvivors.com

National Victims Constitutional Amendment Project (NVCAP)
NVCAP is a 501(c)(4) organization supporting the adoption of an amendment to the U.S. Constitution recognizing the fundamental rights of crime victims to be treated with dignity, fairness, and respect by the criminal justice system.

NVCAP
789 Sherman Street, Suite 670
Denver, CO 80203
Phone: (303) 832-1522
Toll-free: (800) 529-8226
Fax: (303) 861-1265
www.nvcap.org

The Nicole Brown Foundation
"We at the Nicole Brown Foundation pledge our time, our energy and our voices in an effort to educate the national and international communities to the dangers of domestic violence. We help organizations that shelter and protect families in crisis, support long term solutions, and work with educational programs specializing in rehabilitation and job training. We will continue our work until domestic violence is eradicated."

Nicole Brown Charitable Foundation
P.O. Box 3777
Dana Point, CA 92629
Phone: (949) 283-5330
www.nbcf.org

RESOURCES

The Ron Goldman Foundation for Justice

The Ron Goldman Foundation for Justice wishes to empower, inspire, motivate, and assist people who are victims of crime. Our mission is to positively impact the lives of survivors who start each day with pain, grief, trauma, and injustice.

We will strive to offer or connect survivors with all the resources needed to ensure that their path to justice will be more manageable. We will help bring them to a place of strength, courage, determination, and hope in order to better their lives.

The Ron Goldman Foundation for Justice
PO Box 1096
Canyon Country, CA 91386
www.RonGoldmanFoundation.org

Please note: This list is a very small percentage of the thousands of support systems in place to help. Please call or visit their websites to find resources in your neighborhood.